SUSTAIN

Plant-based foods
for active people

Brooke Donoghue, Luuka Jones,
Christel Dunshea-Mooij

BATEMAN
BOOKS

Text © Brooke Francis, Luuka Jones and Christel Dunshea-Mooij, 2022
Photography © Brooke Francis and Luuka Jones
Photos by Juliette Drysdale: 13, 36–7, 49, 53, 56, 60, 67, 72, 191

Page 4 photo by Tim Marshall
Page 21 photo by Steve McArthur, courtesy of Photosport
Page 23 and 28 photos by Marty Melville courtesy of Photosport
Page 25 photo by Fabio Borga
Page 33 and 41 photos by John Cowpland courtesy of Photosport
Page 34 photo by Andrew Cornaga courtesy of Photosport
Page 50 photo by Balint Czucz
Page 68 photo supplied by Jim Webster
Page 79 photo (top left of Ruby Tui) by Kenji Demura courtesy of Photosport
Page 79 photo (top right) by Matty Smith
Page 79 photo (bottom left) by Upstream Films
Page 79 photo (bottom right) by Dom Thomas

Every effort has been made to identify the photographer and copyright holder of
each photograph. Please contact the publisher if any photograph has not been
correctly credited.

The moral rights of the authors have been asserted.

Typographical design © David Bateman Ltd, 2022

Published in 2022 by David Bateman Ltd,
Unit 2/5 Workspace Drive, Hobsonville,
Auckland 0618, New Zealand
www.batemanbooks.co.nz
ISBN: 978-1-77689-034-7

Disclaimer: The information in this book about medical conditions, nutrition and
health is written for informational and educational use only. It does not constitute
medical advice and should not be used as a substitute for medical advice. You
should not use the information in this book for diagnosing or treating a medical
condition, consult a physician in all matters regarding your health. Neither the Publisher nor the Author can be held responsible for any specific individual's reactions, harmful effects or claims arising from the use of the text or the suggestions
it contains, whether in recipe form or otherwise.

A catalogue record for this book is available
from the National Library of New Zealand.

Book design: Megan van Staden
Printed in China through Colorcraft Ltd Hong Kong

Contents

Introduction   5

Fuelling for the work you are doing   9

Getting the best out of yourself   39

SUSTAINability   59

Guest athletes   74

Recipes   81

Index   188

Goodbye   192

Acknowledgements   192

Introduction

Thanks for picking up a copy of *Sustain*. Our aim for this book is to summarise the specific needs of a plant-based diet for athletes, and to provide you with a range of delicious recipes and tips to get the best out of yourself as an athlete.

The recipes in this book aim to sustain us and our sport, as well as the planet and, consequently, future generations. We have often found that vegan and vegetarian diets are assumed to be inadequate for athletes. We want to show you that you can get all you need from a diet with less impact on the environment and still perform at your best.

We also aim to raise awareness of how athletes can choose a plant-based diet and still perform to the highest standards, so our example can benefit the planet and the people around us. You'll find that most of the information is also applicable to anyone striving towards a healthy, balanced life.

As elite athletes, we are so lucky to have an amazing group of support staff around us who are incredibly knowledgeable and skilled, and who push us to get the best out of ourselves. We would like to thank everyone who has contributed to this book. We hope that it is a handy resource that encourages thought and conversation about the topics we cover. We want this book to be a resource of all the things we have learnt to help beginner athletes, weekend warriors, age groupers, elite athletes and beyond.

Remember, everyone has unique nutritional requirements and it is vital to do what is right for you. While this book will provide you with ideas and information about how to make food choices that work best for you, we always recommend you talk with a health professional when making any major changes in your lifestyle.

Finally, we want to encourage you to be mindful in your choices, by considering yourself, others, the planet and to remember that small changes add up.

Sustain — Fuelling for the planet and performance

Charity Support

We feel fortunate to be so well supported in our sporting endeavours. Through sport we have learnt to push ourselves and always aim to be the best versions of ourselves. We have learnt to win, and we have learnt to lose. We have learnt teamwork, communication, and commitment. Each of these skills is invaluable to us in all areas of our lives.

We think everyone should have an opportunity to participate in sport and reap these benefits, which is why we are giving 100 per cent of profits from the sale of this book to The WaterBoy.

The WaterBoy is a charity that breaks down the barriers for youth to participate in sport. These barriers can include financial restrictions, disabilities, lack of confidence, sexuality, age, gender, religion and others. The WaterBoy gives people in these situations the opportunity to participate in sport. This in turn helps to create stronger people and stronger communities.

What is the most important thing in the world?
He tangata, he tangata, he tangata.
It is people, it is people, it is people.

Sponsors

This book would not be possible without the generous backing of our sponsors.

The Moorings, Waiheke Island

The Moorings comprises two luxury studio apartments located in an unbeatable spot over Matiatia Bay in Oneroa, Waiheke Island. Life is all about balance and these studios provide the perfect getaway to enjoy spectacular sunsets and breathtaking sea views. Sometimes it is nice to take a step back from the hustle and bustle of everyday life by breathing in some sea air and relaxing with loved ones.

From the bottom of our hearts, we thank The Moorings for believing in us and bringing our project to life. To see the potential this project has means so much to us. Kia ora.

Brian Perry Charitable Trust

The Brian Perry Charitable Trust has been making a meaningful contribution to the Waikato region for over four decades. The Trust has been instrumental in delivering many community projects including the Te Awa River Ride, the Cambridge Velodrome, and the new Perry Aquatic Centre in Cambridge. It founded and continues to support the Adastra Foundation for athletes and performing artists, and the Perry Outdoor Education Trust.

We are forever grateful for the opportunities and experiences the BPCT have brought to the Waikato community. Your support is not taken for granted and we thank you.

Craigs Investment Partners

Craigs Investment Partners is one of New Zealand's leading investment advisory firms. Craigs operates 19 offices across New Zealand, which support a wide range of community organisations and projects. For Craigs, supporting the community is core to its values, culture and success.

Seeing the diversity of projects supported by Craigs is inspiring. We thank you for backing our book and providing inspiration and support. We hope we can be a small part of a positive change.

Zealandia Horticulture Ltd

Zealandia Horticulture has a long-standing tradition of supporting local communities. It generously supports schools, fairs, gardening projects, the Wairoa River Landcare Society and the Waiora Trust — a community garden that offers friendship and gardening space to people who may be struggling. It also supports multiple sporting events (e.g. the ASB Classic) and the Monarch Butterfly NZ Trust.

Knowing that Zealandia Horticulture is continuously trying to reduce its environmental impact through its growing and business practices (e.g. capturing and reusing water for its plants, using a biomass boiler for heating, producing seedling pots from recycled plastic), we are really thankful for your support, especially as your values are aligned to ours.

Fuelling for the work you are doing

Sport-specific fuelling considerations

Nutrition considerations for the plant-based athlete
Christel Dunshea-Mooij

Worldwide there is a growing interest in plant-based eating patterns that avoid meat or fish, or fully exclude animal products (see figure 1). That is why it is not surprising that more and more athletes, both recreational and elite, are choosing to consume more plant-based protein sources, such as plant-based meat substitutes, legumes, beans, pulses and tofu, and non-dairy milks.

From a global sustainability perspective, plant-based foods are proposed to be advantageous over animal-based foods. The production of plant-based foods generally requires less water, land, and energy than animal-based food and this may ultimately pose less of an environmental burden and lower the cost of production. The growing trend in Western societies of people consuming more plant-based diets is partly due to these concerns. It is important to note that, historically, most of the dietary protein consumed worldwide is already derived from plant-based sources rather than animal-based (58 per cent versus 42 per cent, respectively; see figure 2). So, eating a predominantly plant-based diet is a shift in proportion of plant protein in the diet, not a totally new approach to consumption.

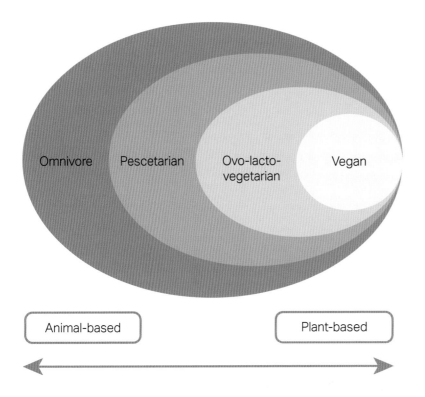

Fig 1: The spectrum of diets*
From left to right: including all food items (omnivore); excluding meat other than fish (pescetarian); excluding meat and fish (ovo-lacto-vegetarian); consuming only plant-based items (vegan)

* Adapted from 'The effects of plant-based diets on the body and the brain: a systematic review' (ncbi.nlm.nih.gov/pmc/articles/PMC6742661/)

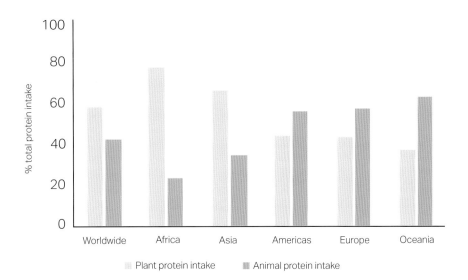

% total protein intake

Worldwide · Africa · Asia · Americas · Europe · Oceania

Plant protein intake   Animal protein intake

Fig 2: The percentage of dietary protein intake derived from plant and animal protein sources in different parts of the world*

* FOASTAT Food Balance Sheets; FAO UN Statistics Division; FOASTAT: Rome, Italy, 2009.

Initiatives such as Meatless Monday — a campaign to encourage people to eat a vegetarian or vegan diet one day a week — and the increase in visibility and availability of vegetarian websites, cookbooks, and vegetarian meals in supermarkets and restaurants are helping popularise plant-based diets. Many international and national organisations — such as the World Cancer Research Fund, NZ Heart Foundation and the New Zealand Nutrition Foundation — recommend consuming a plant-based diet focused on fruit and vegetables, wholegrains and limited animal products for a reduction in the risk of lifestyle diseases. For example, research on dietary patterns[1] shows that vegan and vegetarian diets are associated with a lower risk of heart disease, lower blood pressure[2] and lower low-density lipoprotein (LDL) cholesterol than non-vegetarians.[3]

Vegetarian and vegan diets can be healthy and nutritionally adequate and there is no evidence that there is a difference in athletic performance between vegetarians and non-vegetarians. But it is extremely important that these diets, especially vegan, are planned to provide you with adequate macro nutrients (carbohydrate, fat, and protein) and micronutrients (vitamins and minerals) to support your training and competition. If you are considering switching to a vegetarian diet from a previously omnivorous one, we strongly recommend discussing the reasons behind your decisions with your family, coach, or any other support person to ensure that your decision is warranted and, if necessary, will be supported. There are significant social changes in a vegetarian or vegan diet that

1   Dietary patterns and the heart (heartfoundation.org.nz/resources/dietary-patterns-and-the-heart-evidence-paper)
2   Managing high blood pressure (heartfoundation.org.nz/wellbeing/managing-risk/managing-high-blood-pressure)
3   Tong, T., et al. (2019). Risk of Ischamic heart disease and stroke in meat eaters, fish eaters, and vegetarians over 18 years of follow up. Results from the prospective Epic-Oxford study. *British Medical Journal.* 366:489

Fig 3: Classification of sports in each discipline*

* Adjusted from 'Recommendations for participation in competitive sports of athletes with arterial hypertension: a position statement from the sports cardiology section of the European Association of Preventive Cardiology' (academic.oup.com/eurheartj/article/39/40/3664/5079290?)

may impact your family or close friends and it is important to be clear about your choice and the reasons for it.

We also recommend incorporating ongoing investigations (e.g. analysing blood and other monitoring) following your change in diet to ensure that you are consuming the required daily energy and protein you require as an athlete. Levels of micronutrients, such as iron, can be affected and may need to be monitored.

Vegetarian athletes tend to consume large amounts of cereals, pulses, nuts, fruits and vegetables, which are high in nutrient-rich carbohydrates, unsaturated fats, fibre and magnesium and vitamins C and E, as well as certain phytochemicals that can encourage improved muscle refuelling during periods of strenuous training. Most vegetarian diets meet daily protein requirements, even considering the additional demands recommended for athletes competing in high-level sports. Protein sources include beans, nuts, tofu and wholegrains as well as meat substitutes. The building muscle with plant-based foods chapter (see page 24) will describe in detail how to spread out protein

consumption throughout the day to improve recovery and performance.

Vegetarian diets tend to be low in energy, protein, and fat and meals may need to be of greater volume to meet nutritional demands. We will describe how this can be managed in depth in the eating for the work you are doing chapter (see page 18).

An optimal vegetarian diet will differ depending on whether you are a soccer player, a powerlifter, a rower, an 800-metre sprinter or a tennis player. To maximise performance and recovery, each athlete needs to eat differently based on their sport. The following chapters will provide you with examples for each sport discipline, skill, power, mixed and endurance.

Christel Dunshea-Mooij

Senior performance nutritionist, High Performance Sport New Zealand (HPSNZ)

Before we delve into the nitty gritty, here is the low-down on our expert nutritionist, Christel, to help understand the passion behind the science.

Twenty-three years ago, my now husband ran the London Marathon (2 hours 53 minutes). He made a side trip to Holland to catch up with an old friend and met me. Luckily for me, he took me back to the beautiful land of Aotearoa as a souvenir. We settled in Auckland and now have two amazing sons.

In the Netherlands I worked in health promotion. During this period (1995-1997), it was widely known that many of the lifestyle diseases are prevented by making balanced dietary choices. After settling in New Zealand, I decided to do some further study and enrolled for my Masters of Nutritional Science at Massey University. For my masters project, Games Galore — a feasibility study to investigate the effect of a physical activity and nutrition education programme for 10- to 14-year-old New Zealand overweight and obese children — I combined health promotion with sport to investigate a suitable intervention specific for the New Zealand environment. This took a little longer than anticipated as I was also raising our two young, active boys.

After working for the Clinical Trials Research Unit (Auckland University), doing some lecturing for AUT, and running a private practice with Nikki Hart, I started working for High Performance Sport NZ in 2010. Since starting work in HPSNZ, I have been fortunate to work with many athletes from different sporting codes (e.g. canoe and women's hockey). Currently I am the lead performance nutritionist for Rowing NZ, Sailing NZ and provide nutrition services to my co-author, canoe slalom athlete Luuka Jones. I have been a NZ Registered Nutritionist since 2002 and have an IOC Diploma in Sports Nutrition. My passion for sport developed during my formative years, and I have been lucky enough to represent the Netherlands as a rower.

Working with high-performance athletes is a real privilege. I absolutely love working with a bunch of humble, resilient and focused people who have an intrinsic sense of optimism, are really motivated, have an inner desire to succeed and perform to their best effort each and every time, and also have the ability to set realistic, achievable goals, and then to work hard to attain those goals one step at a time. The athletes I work with are aware that in the process of achieving their goals it is crucial to ensure that they are hydrating and fuelling well, as good nutrition makes the difference between a good athlete and a great athlete. Their open mindset, ability to take criticism at every opportunity and learning from it is inspirational.

During my career I have been lucky enough to support Rowing NZ athletes with their nutrition and hydration requirements at location during their pinnacle events: World Championship (Karapiro, Bled, Chanju) and the London Olympic Games (2012), Rio Olympic Games (2016) and Tokyo Olympic Games (2021). It is an understatement to say that an Olympic Games environment is an interesting one, it's not often you come across a situation where 11,000 athletes are in the same place all needing to sleep, eat, train and perform.

The key to a successful campaign is the planning done prior to the event. At Rowing NZ, we are lucky to work with operations manager Lisa Holton who continuously motivates us to think outside the square. Rio was an interesting environment and we often had to revert to our third contingency plan due to poor hygiene, contaminated water and long commute times that affected efficient nutrient timing. However, the Tokyo Olympics were a totally different ballgame. Assisting athletes with their hydration and fuelling during the hottest games on record, without the ability to go to the supermarket, required some innovative thinking from our amazing team.

Whenever and wherever possible I try to incorporate products that are good for performance as well as the environment. However, working in sport this is not always an easy task. The torchbearer during the opening ceremony of the Tokyo Olympic games wore a uniform made from discarded Coca-Cola bottles and held a hydrogen-fuelled torch formed of repurposed aluminium from disaster relief shelters. We were sleeping on recycled cardboard beds and Brooke received a medal made from old smartphones on a podium 3D-printed from household plastic waste. Despite these efforts there is still loads of waste and there is still lots of work to be done.

One of my main drivers is to educate athletes to fuel and nourish their bodies according to the work they are doing, based on their individual choices and beliefs (e.g. animal welfare, sustainability, religion etc.). My intended approach is to combine the latest evidence-based science with the nutrition needs of the athlete to create an individualised evidence-based nutrition plan. The aim is to optimally nourish the athletes for health and performance and try to debunk fad diets and pseudoscience. When Luuka told me that we were going to write this book I was initially reluctant. But during this last year I have really enjoyed the time spent discussing this project with Brooke and Luuka as it includes so many aspects that are important to me: growing your own vegetables, reducing your footprint, looking after our planet, fuelling and nourishing your body. Hopefully you enjoy reading this book and cooking the recipes as much as we enjoyed creating this resource.

Brooke Francis, née Donoghue

World champion rower, silver medallist Tokyo Olympics

I grew up on a dairy farm in Waiterimu, which is a small rural area in North Waikato. I had a typical Kiwi upbringing and was often helping mum and dad on the farm when I wasn't at school or sports practice. I was keen on sport from a young age, and my interest only grew as I got older. I tried as many sports as I could throughout my schooling. In my last few years of college, I juggled hockey, netball and women's rugby over the winter. It was rowing that really caught my attention, though. Perhaps because I wasn't allowed to start until I was able to drive myself to training, which made me that much keener to do it.

In my last three years of school, I made the decision to adopt a vegetarian diet. I was quite strict on what I ate and would not touch food that had any animal ingredients in it; I did, however, occasionally eat eggs. For me this felt right. I was not comfortable with eating animals, often processed, and I really didn't enjoy the taste. My biggest downfall over these years was not having the education to get what my body needed from food. I slowly became iron-deficient, which came to full fruition when I raced at the Maadi Cup in 2012 and felt completely drained during racing, despite all the good training I had done.

As a teenager, I really hadn't put much thought into what I was eating. I would just eat whatever I felt like when I was hungry and didn't consider protein, carbohydrate, and other nutritional elements my body needed to function well. So, when I left school with a goal to represent New Zealand in rowing, I had to listen to my body, and I decided to eat meat again. I knew my body needed it and I was very passionate about rowing so I wanted to do everything I could to succeed.

Over the next few years of my rowing career, I made a big shift in my performance and recovery by fuelling and sleeping better. This meant I was able to train more consistently and get more out of every performance. We often talk about doing the little things well; without doing these key things improvements are hard to find.

Eating meat and animal products still played on my mind and didn't sit right with me. I reached a point in 2017 where I made the decision to adopt a flexitarian diet and only eat meat when it was given to me, so I could be polite and not turn down food. I used this time to educate myself about how much protein and iron was in the food I was eating. I also used this time to do dietary analysis with my nutritionist to make sure I was eating enough food for the training we were doing — an important exercise to carry out whether you eat meat or not. By 2018, I had gone fully vegetarian and had enough confidence in myself to do it, knowing full well the risks it had for both my performance and my goal of winning gold at the Olympics if I did not eat and manage myself well.

This time round it was not just eating animals that put me off. I had been studying business sustainability at university and the more I learnt about the impact humans have on the planet, the more I wanted to do to help. Eating less meat is proven to be one of the biggest things we can do individually to help reduce emissions and to reduce our impact on our planet.[4] I have been conscious to make an effort around the way I live and to be mindful in my usage of the earth's precious resources.

Rowing has led me on a journey where I want to constantly improve and push myself, which I try to carry into other aspects of my life. In this somewhat selfish journey, I want to do all I can to help those around me and leave the world in a better state than when I found it. Hence why I jumped at the chance to create this book with Luuka and Christel. I hope that this resource helps, inspires, and leaves people's bellies full, whether you adopt a full vegan/vegetarian diet or a conscious flexitarian approach.

4   Eat less meat: UN climate-change report calls for change to human diet (nature.com/articles/d41586-019-02409-7)

Eating for the work you are doing
Christel Dunshea-Mooij

Endurance athletes generally participate in sporting activities of 90 minutes or longer, even over 24 hours. Additionally, endurance athletes can have markedly different body compositions, with vast differences in lean and/or fat mass, from ultra-distance runners (lowish lean and low fat mass) to rowers (high lean and low fat mass).

It is important to individualise the goals of the athlete to their specific sport. Brooke is an endurance athlete. To sustain large power outputs over the duration of a 2km (about 6 minutes) rowing race, Brooke needs to complete large volumes of training. It is crucial that she consumes sufficient calories for the work that she is doing. Failing to do this can put Brooke at risk for relative energy deficiency in sport (RED-S).

RED-S was first recognised by the International Olympic Committee (IOC) in 2014. RED-S is a syndrome that encompasses a myriad of negative impacts caused by energy deficiency for both male and female athletes. RED-S includes, but is not limited to, impairments of metabolic rate, menstrual function, cardiovascular health, loss of muscle mass, loss of bone density, increased risk of fatigue, injury and illness. The underlying factor of this syndrome is caused by low energy availability.

Energy availability is described as the energy available to the body (from food) after the costs of exercise have been accounted for. It is the fuel available for physiological processes within the body.

When energy availability is insufficient to support training, day-to-day physiological processes and important bodily functions, health and performance can be compromised. This causes the body to slow down or stop physiological processes that are not crucial for life, such as reproduction. Vegetarian athletes might struggle to meet their energy needs due to the high fibre content of plant-based diets, especially if this plant-based diet is combined with elevated energy needs and/or hectic schedules that prohibit adequate time to eat.

The increase of prevalence of RED-S among vegetarians is often unintentional and due to the selection of low energy-dense, high-fibre plant foods coupled with high training demands. This can result in decreased sex hormones (including estrogen, progresterone and testosterone). Lower circulating estrogen concentrations in vegetarians compared with non-vegetarian could be due to the higher fibre and lower fat in most plant-based diets.

The signs and symptoms of low energy availability vary from athlete to athlete. Some common symptoms may include excessive fatigue, muscle loss, frequent illness or injury, stress fractures, menstrual dysfunction, inability to recover, and decrease in performance.

Athletes with high energy needs (e.g. endurance athletes) should eat frequent meals and snacks (i.e. five to eight meals or snacks per day) and plan so that food and snacks are readily available. This will help prevent injury, promote growth, and boost overall performance.

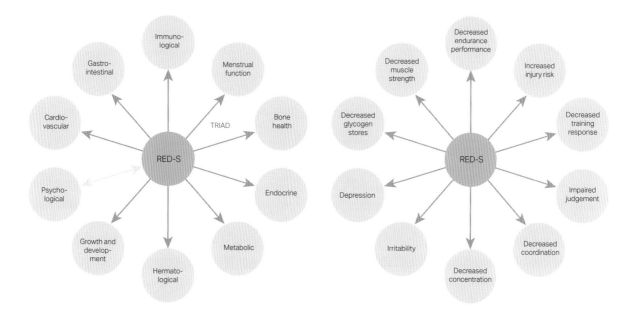

Fig 4: The figure on the left shows the myriad negative health impacts of RED-S. The figure on the right shows the negative impacts of under fueling on performance*

* 'The IOC consensus statement: beyond the Female Triad — Relative Energy Deficiency in Sport (RED-S)' (https://pubmed.ncbi.nlm.nih.gov/24620037/)

BE AWARE OF THE ENERGY COST OF YOUR TRAINING SESSION:

- Most athletes do not increase their food intake when the intensity or duration or their training is increased.
- Athletes' energy requirements change from day to day and across the season. If you follow a basic nutrition plan by eating the same thing every day, your energy availability could be inadequate.
- It is also important to estimate what you are doing outside your training, for example biking to/from training sessions, or certain physical jobs — not incorporating this could lead to a state of low energy availability.
- Athletes often assume that you lose weight if you are not fuelling enough. This is not the case as our bodies are smartly designed to defend against any perceived starvation by slowing down your metabolism.
- Plant-based diets are used by some athletes as a socially acceptable way to restrict energy intake. It is not uncommon to reduce animal food without replacing this with the appropriate plant-based alternatives. This is not recommended.

This is a sample of Brooke's daily food intake. Due to Brooke's high energy expenditure (energy cost of training) she must consume a lot of calories. When her training load decreases, she will eat less (e.g. reduce portion sizes or adjust food intake around training sessions). If Brooke's training load increases, she will have to eat more than the below example (e.g. add supper and increase fuel around training).

Meal	Food	Energy (kcal)
Breakfast	2 slices wholegrain toast + 2 tbsp butter + 2 tbsp peanut butter + 395 ml juice	871 kcal
During morning training (approx. 2 hours)	1 gel and 750 ml sports hydrate	290 kcal (72 g carbohydrates)
Immediately post training	2 slices wholegrain toast + 2 tbsp butter + 3 scrambled eggs + handful spinach leaves + 1 long black + 395 ml juice	789 kcal
Lunch	1 cup oats + 1 tbsp chia seeds + 3 tbsp shredded coconut + ½ cup berries + 1 cup milk	800 kcal
Pre-training snack	Large banana + pot of Greek yoghurt	386 kcal
Weight training	Water during the session	
Recovery	Protein shake (third-party tested) made with milk + 2 multigrain Ryvita crackers with hummus and tomato	373 kcal
Dinner	2.5 cups Kūmara, Lentil and Halloumi Pie (see page 138) + green salad	1080 kcal
Snack	4 squares dark chocolate + peppermint tea	235 kcal
		4824 kcal

Table 1: Example of Brooke's daily energy intake (Christel Dunshea-Mooij)

Luuka Jones

Canoe slalom athlete, four-time Olympian, silver medallist Rio Olympics

Not a single creature on earth has more or less right to be here than you or me.
— Anthony D Williams

My pet chickens were a large part of my decision to become a vegetarian. Spending time with my feathered, free-ranging friends, I realised that these birds feel emotion, love listening to music and are loyal companions. It is in their nature to roam, scratch for insects and to be outside. Unfortunately, for most chickens, they will never get the opportunity to do these very things.

I felt that I had a disconnect between the food on my plate and where it actually came from. It is easy not to have to think about the lives that some of those animals endured to be our next meal. Now, I am very conscious about what I eat and where it comes from. I think, in general, this consciousness is important when it comes to eating.

I held off becoming a vegetarian, because I thought an absence of meat in my diet would negatively affect my performance. I had grown up believing that you had to eat meat in order to train to a high level, and I had always struggled with low iron levels. I spoke about it with my nutritionist Christel and identified ways in which to fuel my training on a vegetarian diet.

Whilst nutrition is only one part of performance, in 2020 my numbers in the gym increased, as well as my testing results on the water. I felt good about my decision to transition to a vegetarian diet, and it had no negative effects. I am confident now that it is absolutely possible as an athlete to fuel for both the planet and performance. Following a vegetarian diet as an athlete does take more planning and thought to ensure that you are getting everything you need. There is also less variety when eating out, however it is something that I am now used to.

Over the years I have learnt that sports nutrition is about consistency. It is about learning what your body needs, what works for you and then ensuring you are fuelling well every day. Preparing recovery smoothies to take to training and ensuring that meals are well timed means you have energy to get the most out of sessions. It is not something I have always been good at, but for me it is a constant process of trying to be better every day.

In the last year, my chickens have taught me that we can pursue our sport, whilst being kind to the creatures that share our planet with us.

Building muscle with plant-based foods

Christel Dunshea-Mooij

Luuka is a strength and power athlete. Strength and power athletes compete in sporting activities that take as little as a few seconds to complete, could last longer than several minutes, and/or could be intermittent in nature. Also, strength and power athletes can have very different lean and/or fat mass. For example, a sumo wrestler has a high lean mass as well as a high fat mass, whereas a slalom canoe athlete has a high lean mass and a low fat mass. This shows that the nutritional needs of strength and power athletes are unique to the body type of the individual athlete as well as the specific sport. Due to the high lean muscle mass required in strength and power sports, most athletes will have a desire to maintain or build muscle mass.

Many strength and power athletes traditionally choose a diet high in protein. While their protein needs are greater than that of non-athletes, they are not as high as commonly perceived. Recommended protein levels to support muscle recovery and adaptation are easily achieved within a normal diet, so many athletes ingest far greater amounts than required. We can safely conclude that the quantity of daily protein intake is not an issue with most strength and power athletes (including athletes opting for plant-based protein sources).

Recovery post exercise

Muscle growth only happens when exercise and nutrition are combined. It is crucial to optimise the dose, type, and timing of protein ingestion as it plays a critical role in promoting protein synthesis. It is strongly recommended to eat 20 grams of high-quality protein within two hours of exercise, either by itself or with carbohydrates, to improve muscle repair and growth. High-quality protein (8-10 grams of essential amino acids per 20 grams) are best for this purpose. Essential amino acids are the building blocks of proteins. These cannot be produced by our bodies and must be consumed from the diet. An athlete needs to eat enough protein to ensure they get all the essential amino acids.

Plant-based protein contains less essential amino acids compared to animal-based proteins. But with a little planning an athlete choosing to consume plant-based foods can easily consume sufficient, good-quality protein from only plant-based sources.

To increase muscle growth, it is crucial that your recovery meal contains enough of the essential amino acid leucine. Leucine is the 'king' that turns on muscle growth for 1-2 hours after you have had a leucine-rich meal. Figure 5 shows the leucine concentrations of various protein sources (plant- and animal-based protein sources).

Optimising protein intake

Muscle (protein) is in a constant state of turnover. Athletes gain muscle mass when they synthesise more muscle protein (muscle protein synthesis) than they break down

Piera Hudson

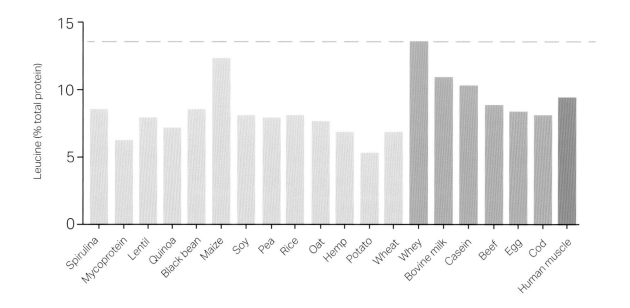

(muscle protein breakdown). Muscle protein synthesis is stimulated by eating protein-rich foods and exercising. Muscle protein breakdown is increased when you do nothing (e.g. during rest and injury) and starvation.

In New Zealand our protein consumption is often skewed heavily towards the evening. Consumption of 20 grams protein spread over a day with snacks or small meals helps stimulate muscle growth and reduce muscle breakdown more effectively than when intake is skewed towards the evening. While protein is important to build muscle mass, more is not necessarily better. Simply eating large amounts of lean protein does not equate to a toned body. When determining your protein requirements, it is important to look at your overall eating pattern.

Fig 5: The leucine concentrations of various protein sources (plant- and animal-based protein sources). The dashed line provides a comparison of the protein source most abundant in leucine (i.e. whey) with the various other protein sources.*

* The Skeletal Muscle Anabolic Response to Plant-versus Animal-based Protein Consumption' (academic.oup.com/jn/article/145/9/1981/4585688?)

Proteins can be used for fuel as well as muscle growth, therefore the amount of carbohydrates consumed affects how much protein can go toward building and maintaining lean body mass. Athletes need to ensure that they are also meeting their needs for carbohydrate and fat, not just protein.

This is an example of Luuka's daily food intake.
To optimise muscle growth and recovery Luuka aims to consume 20 g of protein (body weight X 0.3 g) every couple of hours to assure that she gets the most out of every training session.

Meal	Food	Protein (g)
Breakfast (pre-training)	Overnight oats: 1 cup oats + ½ cup blueberries + ¼ cup walnuts + 1 tsp cinnamon + 1¼ cups milk	27 g
Weight session	Water during the session	
Immediately post-training	Protein shake (third-party tested) made with milk and a banana — *includes plenty of leucine*	34 g
Lunch	Big bowl of Tofu Noodle Soup (see page 110)	25 g
On-water session	Sip on sports hydrate	
Recovery	Peanut Butter Smoothie (see page 88) — *includes plenty of leucine*	24 g
Dinner	Black Bean and Salsa Enchiladas (see page 140)	34 g
Supper	Chia Pudding (see page 84)	17 g

Table 2: Example of Luuka's meal plan spreading approximately 20 g of protein throughout the day (Christel Dunshea-Mooij)

Alexandra Maloney
High-performing sailor, silver medallist Rio Olympics

Alex is a legendary Kiwi sailor, winning a silver medal at the Rio Olympics in the 49erFX event.

Can you tell us a little about yourself?
I love sailing, competitively and for the enjoyment of the activity. Outside of racing, I also enjoy sailing! Sailing other classes of boats is almost like a different sport [and I also enjoy] going cruising with friends and family on keelboats. If not on the water sailing, I enjoy hiking, paddle-boarding, catching up with friends and reading.

How did you come to be a vegetarian?
I have never liked meat from a very young age, which was actually an anomaly from the rest of the Maloney family. When I was five, we moved onto a boat to cruise the South Pacific for a few years, and quality meat wasn't always readily available. So that solidified my avoidance of the food group. There must have been some sort of personal moral compass guiding me away from it too, as I also loved animals and would cry if our family killed a fish we caught from the boat . . . which is now a little embarrassing when Mum tells the story! Later, when we eventually moved onto land in the far north, I didn't grow an appetite for it, so I naturally became vegetarian.

Do you have any tips for travelling around the world whilst being a vegetarian?
Molly, my teammate, isn't vegetarian and we often cook meals for each other when on the road, so we have both learnt how to make a vegetarian alternative to the main meal. It's super easy if you are prepared with lentils, chickpeas, beans or other vegetarian sources of protein. Substituting these staples into a meal and having two pans going on the stove top, is no hassle. Another tip is to bring a bag of nuts (as well as other veggie snacks!) on the plane or road trip, so you have an easy source of protein to reach for.

What is your favourite way to enjoy food?
Fresh, and cooked with friends and family. Eating is a social activity when you're not on the go, and I think when you make the time to slow down to cook well, and enjoy your food, it makes it taste better too.

Effective decision-making for plant-based athletes

Christel Dunshea-Mooij

Alex is a skill-based athlete. Skill-based athletes must demonstrate high effectiveness, high efficiency, and high responsiveness to be able to be successful in their chosen sport. Athletes achieve high effectiveness by being accurate (e.g. sailing the boat where you would like it to go), being consistent (e.g. consistent performances over a regatta week), being controlled (e.g. focus and concentration), and being confident (e.g. belief in their ability). There are a variety of different nutritional requirements for skill-based athletes between and within sports. But due to the effectiveness, efficiency and responsiveness required for athletes competing in skill-based sports, most athletes will have a desire to improve their cognitive functioning.

Plant-based diets are naturally low in several important brain nutrients: vitamin B12, haem iron, creatine, carnosine, taurine, and some omega-3 fatty acids. Many of these nutrients can be manufactured in the lab or extracted from sources such as algae, bacteria, or lichen, and added to supplements. The body can make some of the vital brain compounds from other ingredients in our diets. Some brain compounds are found in plant-based foods, but only in meagre amounts. For example, to get the minimum amount of vitamin B6 required each day from one of the richest plant sources, potatoes, you would have to eat about five cups of potatoes each day. Carefully planning your diet to ensure that you consume sufficient of the important brain nutrients is recommended to ensure that your cognitive function is not compromised.

One of the most well-known challenges for vegans is getting enough vitamin B12, which is found in animal products such as eggs and meat. Other species acquire their B12 from bacteria that live in their digestive tracts or faeces; they either absorb it directly or ingest it by snacking on their own poo, but unfortunately (or fortunately, depending on how you look at it), humans can't do either. If your vitamin B12 levels are low your neurological and cognitive health is compromised.

Iron deficiency can affect optimal cognitive functioning in skill-based athletes due to an undersupply of blood to the brain which reduces the athlete's attention span, ability to learn new things, affect memory, and cause fatigue. More information about iron and B12 can be found on pages 52–55.

Another important nutrient for the brain's functioning is creatine, which can improve memory and reduce mental fatigue. Vegans and vegetarians have significantly lower levels of creatine in their bodies than omnivores, because plants and fungi don't contain any. However, as the brain largely makes its own creatine supply it is currently not clear if vegans need the extra creatine omnivores get from their diets.

Omega-3 fatty acids are components

of all cell membranes, have powerful anti-inflammatory functions within the body and are vital for our normal brain functioning, mental health, and brain development through all stages of life. Low levels of omega-3 fatty acids accelerate brain ageing and contribute to decreased brain functioning.

There are three different types of omega-3 fatty acids: alpha-linolenic acid (ALA), docosahexaenoic acid (DHA) and eicosapentaenoic acid (EPA). You can find ALA in plants (sunflower seeds, cold-pressed sunflower oil, pumpkin seeds, sesame seeds and walnuts), but dietary sources of DHA and EPA are only found in fatty fish such as salmon, mackerel and trout, and shellfish such as mussels, oysters and crabs. If you choose to exclude fish from your diet you need to carefully consider how to replace these crucial nutrients.

It is hypothesised that the amino acid taurine influences mental and athletic performance, which is why it is included in many energy drinks at high levels. Taurine is found in several areas of the body, including the brain, heart and skeletal muscle. The main dietary sources include dairy products, meat and seafood. There is not enough evidence to know what the exact role of taurine is, whether it does in fact give an immediate cognitive boost as claimed by energy drink companies, or if plant-based athletes should supplement taurine into their diet.

Best practice is for all athletes to monitor their health status with frequent blood tests, and to consult a registered performance nutritionist to live healthily on a plant-based diet and avoid nutrient deficiencies or nutrient-overdose-related toxicity.

There is a relationship between mental health and restrictive eating patterns. Carefully planning a plant-based diet and replacing animal food with plant-based alternatives is crucial for optimising your mental health.

Marcus Daniell
World-class tennis player, bronze medallist Tokyo Olympics

Marcus Daniell is world class on and off the court. We admire his passion for sport and his willingness to give back to the community.

Can you tell us a little about yourself?
I'm a doubles player on the Association of Tennis Professionals (ATP) world tour. I've played the Olympics for New Zealand, have competed out numerous Davis Cups, have made Wimbledon and Australian Open quarter-finals, and currently hold five ATP titles. Off court, I'm completing a Master of Philosophy at Massey University and am running a non-profit organisation called High Impact Athletes, which channels donations to the most effective, evidence-based impactful charities in the world. I'm also currently a member of the ATP Player Council alongside Roger Federer, Rafael Nadal, Andy Murray, and five others.

How did you come to be a vegetarian?
Vegetarianism has been in my periphery since I read an environmental philosophy paper at the age of 22. At that point I convinced myself that athletes needed meat, but couldn't deny how compelling the arguments for vegetarianism were. Then, when I was around 27, I went to a fancy sushi restaurant in Tokyo with a few other tennis players, one of whom knew the chef and so was ordering for the table. We'd had some delicious rounds of sushi and were enjoying ourselves, and then he ordered a chopped whale and something inside me instantly rebelled. Whales were sacred and not to be eaten. I didn't partake and got ribbed for it. But on the walk back to my hotel room I knew something had radically changed for me — I suddenly saw the cognitive dissonance between feeling okay eating a cow or a pig or a chicken, but not feeling okay eating a whale. When I examined that more closely, I couldn't think of any valid reason why one was okay to eat and the other wasn't — if all of those animals can feel pain and joy, then all of them deserve a fair shot at life. This shook me, and I started reading deeply into the ethical and environmental implications of eating meat. The more I learnt, the more I realised I couldn't keep doing it. I stopped eating meat the week after and haven't eaten any since.

Do you find it difficult travelling and competing overseas as a vegetarian?
I've learnt that it can be very difficult to find complete vegetarian meals in some of the countries where you'd expect to eat well, like France.

What aspects do you enjoy most about food?
I love experimenting with making my own versions of vegetarian protein like seitan, and I love cooking for groups of my friends and enjoying a glass of wine.

Brooke Neal

Be prepared!
Christel Dunshea-Mooij

Marcus Daniell is a tennis player and for his sport he must travel often to competitions overseas. Although travel is crucial for the individual athletes and to improve the standard of the sport, it raises a whole set of nutritional challenges for them.

There are strategies that plant-based travelling athletes should consider to ensure that they optimise the gains from the experience and maximise the value of the large financial commitment.

Good preparation solves many of the challenges of travel. The athlete will need to follow a balanced nutrition plan while away, but many elements of this plan might have to be organised ahead of time. Prior to departure the athlete should take time to consider the issues likely to be faced on the trip and familiarise themselves with the plant-based options available at the destination. Some countries have ample plant-based options available whereas others only have limited choices. If plant-based options are likely to be absent or in short supply, consider packing a travel kit with appropriate options (shelf-stable-tofu, tinned chickpeas, nuts and seeds, milk powder, powdered liquid meal supplements, third-party tested protein powder, etc.).

The challenge often starts before the athlete arrives at their destination as travelling itself is stressful and changes both the nutritional needs (e.g. changes in activity levels, increased fluid losses in artificial environments) and the opportunities to eat. This is especially important for the athlete who is constantly on the road.

- The air-conditioned environments of trains and buses and the pressurised cabins in planes increase your fluid losses. Take your own fluid supplies when travelling and drink in appropriate amounts to avoid over- or under-hydration as it is crucial that your hydration is optimal when you arrive at your destination.
- Aim to arrive at your destination in the best shape possible by designing a travel eating plan that matches your nutritional goals. It is recommended to contact the airline prior to departure to check if they serve vegetarian meals and inquire about potential challenges of food availability (i.e. find out when the meals are served). This gives you a good idea which meals are needed and whether your own snacks are required.
- Pack a vegetarian freeze-dried meal in your hand luggage to cover the possibility of being stuck in an airport or long layovers.

The fun side of travel is immersing yourself in a new culture. Find local ways of achieving your nutritional goals by balancing the 'tried and true' with the adjustments that a new country requires. Try to identify new foods and eating styles that are compatible with your goals whilst adhering to your preference for a plant-based lifestyle.

- Prior to departure, look up vegetarian restaurants at your destination.
- Most restaurants have vegetarian options, if there is nothing on the menu ask the waiter, they are often more than happy to assist.
- The translation of 'vegetarian' might not be useful as in some countries this may still include meals containing chicken or thin slices of meat. Learn how to say 'no meat or no fish' or 'no pork, chicken, eggs or cheese' in the local language.
- Prior to departure look up supermarkets in the area.
- When you arrive at your hotel, request a mini fridge, or empty the mini bar items to store some vegetarian options bought from the local supermarket or brought from home.
- For longer stays, make sure you have a kitchen or a hot plate with pots and pans to ensure that you can prepare home-made meals.

Getting the best out of yourself

The one percenters

Mental health and wellbeing
Brooke Francis and Eve Macfarlane

We believe our health and happiness is driven from the little decisions we make every day; whether that be eating more fruit and vegetables, making time for our friends and family or getting more sleep and exercise.

As athletes, our mental strength is challenged daily. We are consistently asked to push ourselves beyond what is comfortable, as we ride the ups and downs of the sports we love. Taking time to look after our mental wellbeing is crucial for performance. Being able to check in with ourselves and understand our feelings is vital in sustaining life as an athlete.

To build our mental wellbeing, we think it is important to have a balance in our lives. Having time outside of our sporting world is a good way to switch off and gain insight into new things. We often find that catching up with friends and family and enjoying a meal together is a good way to get out of your own head and thought patterns for a while, and always leaves us feeling uplifted.

For many, maintaining mental health is not easy, and it requires constant work. For changes in our lives to be sustainable they must be enjoyable, doable and approachable. It does not have to be all or nothing, so for a lot of people this is not changing everything overnight. We think that building habits and being intentional with your decisions is a good way to build stronger mental health. Just as in sport, this area requires training and dedication.

Often it is the simple things in life that make us happy. How good is growing your own veggies or having a laugh with a friend! Keeping things simple opens us up to the idea that we can live with less. Often, we find that our happiness and consumption patterns do not match up. We are not always happier with more and by living with less we can actually be happier.

All in all, our mental health and wellbeing is so important. The state of our mind can affect how we think, feel and how we act. We need to share our feelings, the good, the bad and the ugly, so we can be supported and support those around us, so we never have to go through things alone.

Eve has written a book with Jonathan Nabbs called *How We Got Happy*. We highly recommend this book for anyone on their own mental health journey or looking to support those around them. It shares stories from 20 young New Zealanders who have overcome depression, sharing their wellness tools of how they got happy. This book can be purchased from howwegothappy.co.nz

A simple life isn't easy, it is intentional!

Feeling joyful, connected and present

Dr Kylie Wilson (PhD), psychology lead, High Performance Sport NZ (HPSNZ)

My work with athletes focuses on the psychological aspects of performance. What I enjoy most is seeing athletes grow their understanding of who they are as people and how they express that deep self-awareness in pursuit of what they are passionate about. Ironically, sport is a context that is rich in threats to an individual's identity. Some of those threats include judgement from others, comparisons with other competitors or teammates, and constant assessment or judgement of your own competence. Navigating these threats requires security in who you are, what's important to you and a belief that you are enough without performance outcomes defining your worth as a person.

The role food plays in nurturing your sense of security is fascinating. Over the years I have observed athletes identifying food as providing them with a sense of readiness to perform, whether that is linked to believing they have enough energy to perform at their best or ticking the boxes of their pre-performance routines. Through memories or past experiences, food also provides us with connection to a place or person, which can influence our sense of security. When I eat certain foods, they take me back to my childhood when I felt safe and protected (and unaware of the judgement-rich environment that was awaiting me). The challenge is that often these types of food pull me away from achieving my current pursuits. This is a tension many athletes hold in their relationship with food and how it impacts them psychologically.

Working with athletes who are really connected to who they are and how they express themselves through their performance leads them to be less attached to past experiences (often unhelpful or painful ones) or future worries and leads them to make choices that serve them in the present. I also notice this freedom promotes attention at each moment, which is a key ingredient for successful performance. Being present may look like spending time preparing and really enjoying eating the food you (or others if you are lucky) have prepared. Who would have thought eating mindfully would equate to visiting the mind gym and building your ability to be present when you are performing?

Athletes tend to view food as fuel for their training and performance, which it often is. However, food is also an expression of who we are, which tends to be based on the relationships we have with people and places. The balance athletes have between using food purely for fuel and as a way to connect to and express who they are is important for psychological health and overall wellbeing. In my own experience, I have been fortunate to work with some amazing humans who happen to be high-performance athletes. Some of our most meaningful work has taken place over a shared meal that grounds us in the present and connects us to something joyful. It is my belief that feeling present and connected are essential ingredients in most meaningful pursuits.

Optimise your recovery to create a harmonious kingdom

Dr Dan Smart (PhD), performance scientist and strength and conditioning coach

While the focus of this book is primarily based on plant-based nutrition and eating to optimise health, wellbeing and performance in athletes, another aspect of the performance puzzle is the physical training. It could be said that diet and nutrition represent the queen while training could be seen as the king in sporting performance. However, both need to be optimised in order to make a harmonious kingdom.

The training process is divided into waves of higher training loads (a combination of volume and intensity), followed by short periods of lower load and recovery to allow optimal physiological adaptation to occur, which is what we call periodised training. If there is insufficient time for recovery, a slump in performance can occur, which can lead to unwanted responses such as overreaching and overtraining.[5]

Over a period of training, for the body to continue to make positive adaptations it requires sufficient stimulus with a disruption of homeostasis over a sustained period. This consistent accumulation of work is required to cause improvements in central and peripheral cardiovascular function and metabolic efficiency in endurance training, and improve neuromuscular activation, increase muscle fibre cross-sectional area and reduce tendon stiffness in strength-

and power-based training. In other words, making the athlete fitter and stronger.[6, 7]

Research has shown that successful endurance athletes spend 80 per cent of their training time below their aerobic threshold — this is where the athlete is working but can still hold a conversation — and 20 per cent above — where a conversation cannot be maintained.[8] From a real-world perspective this means easy training days are easy and hard training days, while hard, are at the appropriately targeted higher intensity and not necessarily maximal.

Typically, in recreational athletes, a common training mistake is the migration of intensity to the middle, i.e. easy is too hard and hard is not hard enough. Similarly, from a strength-training perspective, modulating loads between and within sessions, especially sessions that target similar muscle groups, are required to drive physiological adaptation. This can be achieved by manipulating the percentage of repetition maximum (RM) lifted or overall volume (sets

5   Matos, N., Winsley, R., & Williams, C. (2011). Prevalence of nonfunctional overreaching/overtraining in young English athletes. *Medicine and Science in Sports and Exercise, 43(7).* 1287–1294.

6   Folland, J. & Williams, A. (2007). The adaptations to strength training. Morphological and neurological contributions to increased strength. *Sports Medicine, 37.* 145–168.

7   Laursen, P. (2010). Training for intense exercise performance: high-intensity or high-volume training? *Scandinavian Journal of Medicine and Science in Sports, 20(Supp 2).* 1–10.

8   Seiler, S. (2010). What is best practice for training intensity and duration distribution in endurance athletes? *International Journal of Sports Physiology and Performance, 5.* 276–291.

and reps) to elicit the desired neuromuscular and metabolic stimulus.[9]

Overall, the appropriate periodisation through the balance of different ratios of load and the slow accumulations of workloads, regardless of the modality, is a cornerstone in allowing you to perform more consistent training; and it's this consistency that is key in achieving long-term health and performance increments.

As an aside to appropriately prescribed training, recovery techniques can be used to enhance the ability to back up training and maintain the consistency required. Much research has been done in this field with a wide variety of outcomes in both physiological adaptation and performance. However, from this abundance of research a few clear conclusions have been made.[10]

- Appropriate sleep quality and quantity is reported to be the single best recovery strategy due to its recuperative and restorative effects.
- Hydrotherapy, using cold-water immersion (CWI) or contrast water therapy (CWT — the rotation between hot- and cold-water immersion) has shown beneficial effects for recovery.

The body responds to water immersion with changes in blood flow and peripheral and core temperatures, affecting inflammation, immune function, muscle soreness and perception of fatigue.[11]

- There is minimal evidence to show that compression garments may be beneficial for recovery, however, there does not appear to be harmful effects relating to their use.
- Recovery periods should be planned accordingly as there might be periods during a training cycle where recovery could be minimised to increase fatigue and potential adaptation.

In summary, the accumulation of consistent workloads is required to drive appropriate physiological adaptation. This is primarily achieved through the planned undulation of training load (volume and intensity) to provide suitable stimulus to disrupt homeostasis and ensuring recovery is adequate to return to an improved physiological baseline and create fitter and stronger athletes. In addition, recovery techniques can be used to enhance this process so more consistent training can be performed.

9 Bird, S., Tarpenning, K., & Marino, F. (2005). Designing resistance training programmes to enhance muscular fitness. A review of the acute programme variables. *Sports Medicine, 35.* 841–851.

10 Halson, S., & Argus, C. (2012). Recovery for endurance training and competition. In I. Mujika (Ed), *Endurance Training Science and Practice* (pp.61–71). Inigo Mujika.

11 Halson, S. (2013). Recovery techniques for athletes. *Sport Science Exchange, 26(120).* 1–6.

Beat the heat
Brooke Francis and
Christel Dunshea-Mooij

Brooke and Luuka (and many other athletes in our book) competed at the Tokyo Olympic Games. In Tokyo the temperature ranged from 30-35°C with humidity at around 70 per cent. This means that the perceived or 'feels like' temperature will be around 40-45°C. The heat can take a major toll on our athletes and optimising hydration is crucial to be able to cope with the heat as well as optimising immunity and performance.

The human body is mostly made up of water and keeping well hydrated is vital to keep your body in good working order in the heat. Competing in hot and humid conditions encourages your body to sweat, a process which helps your body cool down. Too much sweating could lead to dehydration, which accelerates the rise in whole-body temperature, and can have a negative influence on health and performance.

Dehydration also causes an increased stress hormone response and reduces saliva flow. As saliva contains several antimicrobial properties helping to improve your immune function, it is crucial to ensure that you keep hydrated before, during and after exercise, particularly if you're exercising at a high intensity for more than 90 minutes. After training or competition in the heat, recovery drinks should include sodium, carbohydrate and, if necessary, protein to optimise recovery. The preferred method of rehydration is through the consumption of fluids with salty foods.

To check if you are well hydrated, aim to pass pale-coloured urine throughout the day. But if you are going to the loo every 5 minutes you might be overdoing it!

Water and sports drinks are usually thought of as some of the better fluids to hydrate or rehydrate. Professor Ron Maughan, a world expert in hydration, compared several different drinks and captured their hydrating properties in the Beverage Hydration Index (BHI). Essentially, the index compares how much of your drink is retained 2 hours after consumption compared to the same amount of water. The higher the index, the more fluid is retained in the body, which is great for any athlete competing in the heat.

The results of this study demonstrated that some drinks had better hydrating properties than water. Perhaps not surprising is the fact that oral rehydration solutions scored the highest value. These heavily researched medical drinks deliver fluid fast, and the high electrolyte content is responsible for fluid retention. But trim milk, whole milk, and orange juice also scored well.

It was surprising to see that beer (lager), coffee and tea had scores that were very similar to water. They certainly did not display the dehydrating properties that are often talked about. It is likely that the dehydrating properties of alcohol and caffeine were counterbalanced by the fluid-retaining properties of the other ingredients

Are You Drinking Enough Water?

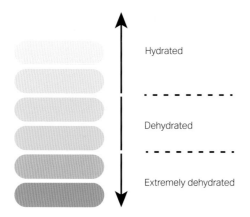

Hydrated

Dehydrated

Extremely dehydrated

Beverage Hydration Index
The higher the value, the better fluid is retained in the body

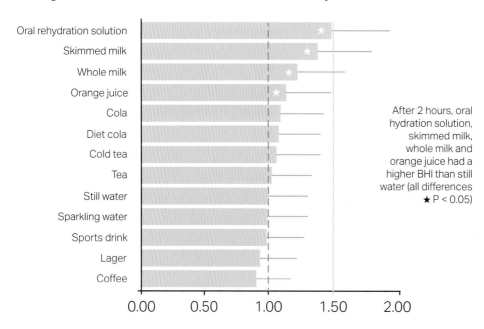

After 2 hours, oral hydration solution, skimmed milk, whole milk and orange juice had a higher BHI than still water (all differences ★ P < 0.05)

in these beverages. Thus alcohol and caffeine in very small amounts do not have diuretic effects (especially for habituated caffeine drinkers).

We can also learn from this study that several beverages were comparable to water (e.g. sports drinks, tea, cola, diet cola). Be aware of the sugar content of sports drinks, juices, cordials, and fizzy drinks, though. They might hydrate as well as water, but they also provide you with lots of calories from sugar, which can contribute to weight gain and poor dental health.

While some drinks are better than others at allowing you to retain fluids, most drinks will contribute to daily fluid requirements. Nonetheless, some fluids will be more appropriate for peak performance than others. In summary, aim to drink plenty of water, depending on your sweat losses, and keep an eye on your urine colour.

As important as it is to think about what liquids we are putting in our bottle, it is also important to consider the vessel we are drinking from. Namely, using and drinking from single-use plastic bottles should be avoided. There are two good reasons for this. It is thought that 14 per cent of all litter is made up of drink bottles. It has been shown that the human population uses 1 million plastic bottles a minute, and this number is rising. This is a huge contributor to the world's plastic waste problem. Even if we think these bottles will be recycled, it is said that only one in six plastic bottles are actually recycled.[12] What is not recycled will likely end up in landfill and take upwards of 450 years to decompose. This is the same for bottles that end up littered on land and in our waterways. These bottles often end up in the ecosystem, which is harmful to wildlife and poses a threat to us humans as microplastic enters the food chain.

The other reason to avoid drinking from single-use plastic bottles is that there can be harmful toxins in the plastic that end up in our bloodstreams. Not all single-use plastic bottles are made to be used again and again. These bottles can also be harder to keep clean and could end up as a harmful breeding ground for bacteria.

To solve this problem, we recommend investing in a good-quality insulated metal bottle. They are easy to clean and can be used again and again. Being insulated also means the bottle will be able to keep your drinks hot or cold for longer.

To avoid even more plastic waste from being produced, we also recommend using tubs of sports hydrate while you train to reduce the need for as many single-use pieces of plastic.

These are small steps but, as more of us adopt them, they can amount to big change.

12 The Facts (plasticoceans.org/the-facts/)

Trust your gut
Brooke Francis and Christel Dunshea-Mooij

Every human harbours anywhere between 10 trillion and 100 trillion microbial cells, with the biggest populations of microbes residing in the gut (about 2 kilograms of micro-organisms). Our gut microbiome is the accumulation of all the micro-organisms that live in our digestive tracts. This includes bacteria, viruses, fungi and other single-celled animals that live in the body.

Estimates vary, but there could be more than 1000 different species of micro-organism making up the gut microbiota. Vegetarian and vegan diets based on legumes, grains, vegetables and fruit are high in fibre, which is great for microbial diversity and health-related bacteria species. A high-fibre diet literally feeds and makes the bacteria thrive. In turn they increase in number and kind. You can compare a high-fibre environment for the gut with good-quality soil that makes seeds grow and thrive. Eating 30 different plant-based foods weekly is good for our gut health by varying our gut bacteria and building a healthier gut microbiome as a result.

Athletes on a plant-based diet have a specific microbial profile because they eat more carbohydrates and therefore ferment more carbohydrates than protein in their gut. This affects different species of micro-organisms in the gastrointestinal tract and leads to a better gut-driven appetite regulation and might help prevent chronic diseases such as obesity and type 2 diabetes and lead to less long-term weight gain.

We have all heard the saying 'trust your gut' or I am sure you've had a gut feeling about something. But did you know that these sayings have come about because your gut is linked to your brain? There are signalling pathways between our gut and brain, called the microbiome-gut-brain axis. Thus, what is happening in our gut can affect our moods, mental health and cognitive function.

Good gut health is important for the functioning of other areas too, including our digestion, immune system, skin health and our general wellbeing.

Here are a few ways to build better gut health:

1. Include lots of probiotic foods in your diet

Probiotic foods naturally have sufficient live and active bacteria to provide a health benefit. When you eat foods that contain probiotics, they make their way down into your gut, where there is an ecosystem of bacteria working hard to help your body stay well. This ecosystem of bacteria is called your gut flora or gut microbiome. In an ideal situation your gut microbiome should be made up of a wide variety of good bacteria because they all play different roles in keeping you healthy.

Probiotic foods include yoghurt (with live cultures) and fermented foods such as kefir, kombucha, sauerkraut, pickles, miso, tempeh, kimchi, sourdough bread and some cheeses.

2. Include lots of prebiotic foods in your diet

It is important to nourish the good bacteria in your gut with lots of prebiotic foods. If probiotics were the flowers in your garden, the prebiotics are the soil for the flowers to thrive in. Prebiotics are broken down by the good bacteria into short chain fatty acids (SCFA). These SCFAs help to keep the lining of your gut healthy, which has been linked with reduced inflammation, increased absorption of nutrients and can protect against certain cancers.

Prebiotic foods include fibre-rich foods such as wholegrains, beans and legumes, fruits, and vegetables.

3. Eat fewer processed foods

Diets that contain a lot of processed food cause an imbalance in the gut microbiome, and lead to many inflammatory diseases.

4. Get enough sleep

Sleep is important for our mood, cognition, and gut health. Not getting enough sleep or suffering from irregular sleep patterns is linked to having negative effects on our gut health. It is important to have good sleep habits by going to bed and getting up at the same time every day.

5. Reduce stress

Stress is good and bad. Good stress includes physical stress from exercise where we put stress on our muscles and vasculature system to strengthen it. Stress can also come in the form of physiological stress, e.g. taking an exam or meeting deadlines at work. A balance needs to be struck here, as too much of either of these can cause unhealthy stress, which leads to an inflammatory response in the body. This results in our gut health and immune system being compromised and less able to fight off illness.

6. Exercise regularly

Exercising regularly is important, especially for our gut health. Regular exercise is important as it tends to keep our bodily functions moving and helps get rid of waste (if you know what we mean!). Having an exercise routine also ties into healthy eating habits, as you'll be motivated to keep hydrated and feed yourself properly to stay fuelled.

Test not guess

Brooke Francis and
Christel Dunshea-Mooij

Vitamins and minerals are essential substances that your body needs to develop and function normally. Athletes should aim to meet their vitamin and mineral requirements through a healthy diet that includes lots of nutrient-dense foods (e.g. wholegrains, fruits, and vegetables). A 'food first' policy should be the basis of an athlete's nutrition plan to get sufficient vitamins (i.e. vitamins A, B, C, D, E, K) and minerals (i.e. calcium, phosphorus, potassium, sodium, chloride, magnesium, iron, zinc, iodine, sulphur, cobalt, copper, fluoride, manganese, and selenium).

Plant-based diets are naturally lower in certain vitamins and minerals than an omnivore diet and athletes on plant-based diets are at a higher risk of being deficient in certain vitamins and minerals. That is why we encourage you to test and not to guess. Analysing bloods and other monitoring will give you an indication whether important micronutrients such as iron and B12 are deficient or sufficient.

A complete dietary analysis by a registered sports nutritionist or dietitian will also identify if you are consuming sufficient vitamins and minerals from your diet. Based on this analysis, you might be encouraged to increase foods that are high in certain vitamins and minerals. Or if a blood test shows that you are deficient you might be advised by your healthcare professional (doctor or nutritionist) to supplement with specific vitamins and minerals.

Sadly, the supplement industry is not well regulated; up to 25 per cent of over-the-counter supplements could contain substances that are banned in sport by the World Anti-Doping Agency (WADA).[13] As athletes are responsible for prohibited substances, metabolites or markers found in their body (it doesn't matter how or why a substance entered the athlete's body) and many supplements do not have adequate quality control or have all the ingredients correctly labelled, it is recommended to choose third-party tested supplements. A third-party tested supplement is manufactured and then sent to an independent and unaffiliated testing company, which then tests the finished supplement for label accuracy and purity. Some third-party testing certification programmes include Informed Sport, NSF International's Certified for Sport, and Human and Supplement Testing Australia (HASTA).

Vitamin B12

Vitamin B12 is hugely important to help form red blood cells and to help the blood carry oxygen through your body, which is essential for energy production. It is also important for neurological and immune

---

13 'Intended or Unintended Doping? A Review of the Presence of Doping Substances in Dietary Supplements Used in Sports' (ncbi.nlm.nih.gov/pmc/articles/PMC5691710/)

function. B12 is most readily available in animal products. As a plant-based athlete you need to be very conscious to include B12-rich foods in your diet.

Sources: fish, milk, cheese, eggs, nutritional yeast, Marmite and other B12-fortified foods

Iron

Iron is crucial for athletes as your body uses iron to make haemoglobin, which is a protein in red blood cells that transports oxygen from the lungs around the body, and myoglobin, which is a protein that provides oxygen to muscles. Iron is also important for hormone function and energy production — you may notice you feel more tired when you are low in iron.

Sources: iron-fortified cereals, fish, shellfish, legumes, nuts, dried apricots, seeds, quinoa and spinach

Magnesium

Magnesium is a co-factor in more than 300 enzyme systems that regulate diverse biochemical reactions in your body, including protein synthesis, muscle contractions, nerve function, blood glucose control, and blood pressure regulation. Magnesium is required for energy production.

Sources: pumpkin seeds, almonds, peanuts, cashews, wholegrains, dark chocolate, legumes, dairy, banana, apple, raisins, broccoli, spinach, skin-on potatoes and peas

Zinc

Zinc is needed for your defensive (immune) system to work properly. It plays a role in cell division, cell growth, wound healing, bone and teeth formation, the breakdown of carbohydrates and is important for your brain and nervous system. Zinc is also needed for the senses of smell and taste.

Sources: shellfish, dairy, eggs, seeds, peanuts, brazil nuts, almonds, wholegrains and oats

Iodine

Iodine is only required in small amounts but is important for thyroid function. Your thyroid gland uses it to make hormones that help control growth, repair damaged cells and support a healthy metabolism.

Sources: seaweed, eggs, iodised table salt and dairy products

Protein-rich foods

Protein is an important building block for building and repairing muscles, bones, cartilage, skin, and blood. Our bodies also use protein to make enzymes, hormones, and other body chemicals. As we discussed in an earlier chapter (see page 26) it is recommended to include a little protein into your diet every 3-4 hours as well as consuming leucine-rich protein after your training session.

Sources: tofu, lentils, chickpeas, quinoa, eggs, nuts, seeds, oats, and chia seeds

Omega-3 fatty acids

In the decision-making chapter (see page 30) we discussed omega-3 fatty acids as they are components of all cell membranes, have powerful anti-inflammatory functions, improve your nervous system, and are vital for normal brain functioning, mental health and brain development. They also help to improve sleep and skin conditions as well as balancing hormones. We mentioned that there are three types of omega-3 fatty acids: (1) alpha-linolenic acid (ALA), (2) docosahexaenoic acid (DHA) and (3) eicosapentaenoic acid (EPA).

Sources: you can find ALA in plants (sunflower seeds, cold pressed sunflower oil, pumpkin seeds, walnuts and sesame seeds) but dietary sources of DHA and EPA are only found in fatty fish such as salmon, mackerel, trout, and shellfish such as mussels, oysters, and crabs.

Probiotics

As we mentioned in the gut health section (see page 48), probiotics are important for introducing good bacteria into our guts. Probiotic foods are generally fermented and help to support our immunity and cognitive function.

Sources: yoghurt, kefir, kombucha, sauerkraut, pickles, miso, tempeh, kimchi, sourdough bread, and some cheeses.

Prebiotic fibre

Also mentioned in our gut health section (see page 48), prebiotic fibre is from foods that promote the growth of beneficial gut microbes. These foods help promote the growth of good bacteria in our guts.

Sources: asparagus, bananas, garlic, onion, and wholegrains

Inflammation
Brooke Francis and Christel Dunshea-Mooij

Inflammation is both good and bad as it is our body's way of protecting itself from infection, illness, and injury. Good inflammation is when our body responds to stress such as when we get a cut, bruise or something that irritates our body. Our body creates an inflammatory response by starting a defence to protect and repair the body. This is a short-term reaction, and our inflammation reduces as we get better. On the other hand, bad inflammation is when the inflammation process goes on for too long or our levels of inflammation are too high. Bad or chronic inflammation is often due to a non-balanced diet, too much weight around the abdominal area, high stress levels, low activity and not enough sleep.

We can reduce inflammation by eating plenty of antioxidant-rich fruit, vegetables, wholegrains, fatty fish, nuts, seeds, legumes, olive oil and turmeric. Ideally, we should aim to reduce foods that cause inflammation — e.g. fried foods, refined carbohydrates, sugary drinks and foods high in saturated fats — to improve our health and wellbeing.

Shifting towards a vegetarian or plant-based diet can naturally help with inflammation in two ways. By reducing the amount of meat and dairy in your diet you'll decrease any inflammation caused by these (potentially) inflammatory foods. Also, a balanced vegetarian or plant-based diet will consist of foods that are naturally high in inflammation-reducing antioxidants.

MENSTRUAL CRAMPS

Eating foods that decrease inflammation in the body just prior to and during your period will help to tame menstrual cramps. These foods include fruits, vegetables, wholegrains, legumes, fish, nut and seeds. Research has shown that both a vegetarian and plant-based eating pattern work to decrease inflammation in the body.[14]

14 Using Foods Against Menstrual Pain (pcrm.org/good-nutrition/nutrition-information/using-foods-against-menstrual-pain)

SUSTAINability

Sustaining your
performance and
the planet

SUSTAINability
Brooke Francis

Sustainability is a word we are hearing more and more. We often hear this word used around environmental issues, as people highlight the challenges the world is facing and realise that urgent action is needed to sustain the world we live in — we cannot continue to consume more than the planet can replenish.

The meaning of sustainability is commonly agreed upon as 'meeting our own needs without compromising the ability of future generations to meet theirs'.

From a climate change perspective, hundreds of countries have signed up to the Paris Agreement; an international treaty outlining a global response to climate change. The agreement ties in with the Sustainable Development Goals set up by the United Nations Global Assembly, which provide a roadmap for climate actions so that countries can work towards reducing emissions and building a climate-resilient future.

As important as the global response is, what we do as individuals is equally important. Sustainability is, in fact, a way of life, where we live intentionally by thinking about how our actions impact ourselves, others and the planet.

For example, in our day we can make many intentional decisions that mean we are not just following the status quo. These include choosing to bike not drive, by supporting local, by buying ethically made clothes, by choosing to consume less and, of course, our decisions around what we eat.

Most of us care about these issues, but sometimes our actions do not reflect this, even though we know better. An example of this was my experience at the Tokyo Olympic Games. So much waste was created for two leading reasons: hygiene and convenience. I definitely fell into a trap of consuming what was convenient, such as getting a drink out of a vending machine rather than filling up my bottle.

My coach, James Coote, talks about us navigating our rowing journey with a compass, rather than a map. We will not always stay on track or rigidly to plan but by using our compass we will always be able to guide ourselves back to the path we want to follow. This rings true to me from a sustainability aspect too. I will always aim to follow the best path, but it is okay to sway off course and not be perfect as long as we stay true to our values and head in the right direction. This journey does not have to be all or nothing.

My friend and fellow rower Eve Macfarlane and I have often discussed sustainability and being more intentional with using the world's resources.

Doing what we can for the environment can sometimes be stressful and it can feel that, individually, we are not able to do enough. But every change does add up, no matter how big or small. We do not know the full extent our actions have on other people and we might just be the catalyst that inspires others to eat less meat or to live with less.

On a side note, at times I have struggled in social situations being vegetarian and having to defend my decision. But it is a choice, and we all need to be accepting and supportive of one another's decisions and give people time to try new things on their own terms.

It can be hard to know where to start on a sustainable journey. For me one of the biggest behaviour changes I made was around the food I eat. One of the most effective ways to lessen our impact on the world is to eat less meat. I was shocked to hear the facts and figures involved in a plant-based diet versus an omnivore diet, especially the impact on land, waterways, and the ocean.

Land

From a land perspective, farming animals for food is resource intensive (uses large areas of land and water) and causes land degradation, particularly where farming is intensive and uses lots of sprays and chemicals.

Livestock farming contributes significantly to global greenhouse gas emissions. Greenhouse gases contribute to global warming. Global warming is a result of an increase of gases that are emitted into the atmosphere. These gases come predominantly from burning fossil fuels for electricity, heat and transport but also come from animal belching. These gases wrap around the earth's atmosphere and trap in the sun's heat, which warms the earth — this is known as the greenhouse effect. The process alone is not the issue — as we need this atmosphere to keep heat in the earth — the problem is that the increase of gases is trapping too much heat in the earth and causing the temperature to rise. This contributes to warmer seas, ice caps melting, species extinction and extreme weather events.

In comparison, according to a UN report on sustainable resource management, eating a plant-based diet is thought to reduce an individual's carbon footprint from food by up to 75 per cent. Going plant based could be the single biggest way you can reduce your environmental impact on the earth and help to preserve it for future generations.

Water

Water is life. Without water, we have no life. Many of us take this natural resource for granted. It often seems unlimited, but that is far from the truth. Of the 1,260,000,000,000,000,000,000 litres of water on earth only 0.3 per cent is usable for humans, the other 99.7 per cent is in the oceans, frozen in ice caps or is floating in the atmosphere.[15]

Therefore, it is so important to conserve and be mindful of our water consumption.

One of the biggest ways we can reduce our water usage is by eating less meat.

---

15 Earth's Freshwater: Full Teacher Guide
(nationalgeographic.org/media/earths-fresh-water/)

Farming animals uses huge amounts of water. For example, it takes 5875 litres/kg to produce lentils compared to 15,415 litres/kg to produce beef.[16]

As athletes, particularly us water-sport athletes, we see first-hand the effects land usage has on our waterways. Water runoff from farms and industrial businesses enters the waterways and we see the effects in poor water quality, and unhealthy habitats for animals and wildlife. What we consume and the businesses we choose to support need to be carefully considered to ensure we do not add to the problem.

As well as choosing not to eat meat or animal products we can make a difference to our water footprint by taking shorter showers, using eco-friendly products that do not impact the environment as they go down the drain, using minimally packaged products to reduce the chance of packaging ending up in our waterways, and by supporting businesses that are also conscious of these issues.

Ocean

Fish are friends not food . . . well for some of us anyway.

This is not to say that people shouldn't eat fish. Fish and seafood is packed full of nutrients such as omega-3, iron, zinc and iodine. Like anything though, I do think it is important to consider where our food comes from and the impact it has on people and the planet.

Many of us have seen the impact human consumption has had on our beaches and coastlines. It is sad to see rubbish washed up on beaches and animals being affected by polluted habitats. My best memories come from being by the water, which I am sure is the same for many others, so ensuring this resource is protected for future generations is crucial.

The ocean is feeling the pressures of excess consumer plastic waste and overfishing. The ocean makes up 70 per cent of our earth's surface and is keeping us alive by producing over half of the world's oxygen while also absorbing 50 times more carbon dioxide than our atmosphere.[17] The ocean also helps regulate our climate by transferring heat from the equator to the poles to regulate our weather patterns.

Those of us who have the privilege of choosing what we consume need to be consuming responsibly. Taking the pressure off this natural resource by reducing our plastic waste, by making sure our waste does not end up in waterways and by choosing to support sustainable fishing will go a long way towards protecting our oceans.

16 How Much Water Does It Take To Produce Your Fave Foods (befresh.ca/blog-how-much-water/)

17 About the UN Ocean Conference (un.org/en/conferences/ocean2022/about)

Happy choices
Dr Jim Webster (PhD), Animal Behaviour and Welfare

Feeling good about the food you have put in your shopping bag is a great benefit of plant-based diets.

When you include animal products in your diet you are mostly relying on intelligent beings with feelings to provide that food and this should be respected. Science continues to reveal animal attributes (chickens can do simple maths!)[18] and it can no longer be denied that animals have emotions, awareness of themselves and feelings. This makes it increasingly challenging to accept raising animals to provide food in conditions that prevent their natural behaviours or cause negative emotions or discomfort.

Some people who consume animal products therefore feel a conflict between the love of the product and concern about how the animals that were killed to produce it were treated. Avoiding animal products does remove this dilemma, but by choosing your animal products wisely you can feel good about the animal and by 'voting' with your wallet even shift production systems to ones that are better for animals in the long term.

The move to large-scale production of cheap animal products has resulted in a decline in the quality of life for the animals in those systems — ultimately the animals paid the price. This has caused concern and increased interest in animal welfare leading to a proliferation of laws, regulations, and guidelines to govern the activities of producers. While this has undoubtedly improved conditions for some animals, progress is still too slow for some people, leaving a gap between expectations for animal care and production conditions, which can lead to tension.

Retailers have stepped into this space, particularly overseas, introducing their own standards of production that can be more stringent than the legal ones. A move to higher-welfare animal products may mean paying more, but this is a resetting to what the cost of ethical production is and what the real value of consuming animal products should be.

Removing yourself from consumption of animal products reduces the demand for those products. Alternatively, if you are comfortable with certain animal products such as milk or eggs, choosing those from high-welfare systems can help shift production practices, as has happened with the increase in cage-free egg production.

The role of retailers and the power of the consumer in changing farming systems should not be underestimated. In these days of 'greenwashing', research by you as the consumer is needed to confirm you are happy with your food choice.

Firstly, think about the retailer, what is their philosophy, have they done any of the work sourcing welfare-friendly products for you (think Whole Foods Market in the USA)?

---

18 Chickens Can Do Math (scienceworld.ca/stories/chickens-can-do-math)

You can always ask them. Secondly, look at the product label: what does it say about the system? Are there any certifications on the label (preferably from a third party such as SPCA rather than an industry body)? Is there a contact number, website address or physical address for the producer? You can call, check out the website, or even drive by.

You can seek out products that allow animals to behave naturally and range freely, and these do tend to come from smaller systems, although smaller systems do not automatically guarantee better welfare for animals. A simple message is do not automatically accept marketing pictures or language on animal products, but check them out for yourself. While this does take effort, if this is an area you care about it can make a difference to your satisfaction and enjoyment and connect you more closely to your food sources.

The egg or the chicken?

Dr Jim Webster (PhD), Animal Behaviour and Welfare

Eggs are a great natural product — they are nutritious and, importantly, do not harm the chicken that produces them. However, when buying eggs, there is an important choice to make that can influence the quality of life of the chicken that laid it.

Chickens are wonderful, intelligent birds that naturally spend most of their time exploring and foraging for food. Modern laying hens evolved from jungle fowl, and while humans have gradually conditioned them to lay more eggs, they still carry behaviours of their ancestors. They have an inbuilt need to forage, scratch, dust bathe and perch. Being a prey species, they have a natural tendency to avoid predators by staying close to overhead cover. This same desire for safety means that when chilling out during the day or at night, they like to perch high off the ground.

While some production systems allow these behaviours, others even restrict the ability of the birds to move about and explore. Chickens have long been farmed in industrial-style systems in cages or in huge groups with little to do once they have eaten the concentrated food sources provided. In these systems, the beaks of the birds are trimmed shortly after hatching to reduce their ability to injure each other as they satisfy their need to forage. The terminology of the production system is important then, and some research when selecting eggs as described above is required. Conventional cages are very restrictive on bird movement and behaviour, so much so that they will be phased out in New Zealand in 2022.

Colony cages are larger and have been designed to keep birds in bigger groups and provide them with more resources to promote natural behaviours (however they are still a 'cage'). 'Barn' systems improve the ability of birds to move but can still have issues due to the size and density of the groups. Free-range systems that give birds access to the outdoors will help promote more natural, richer lives, although we need to accept that the great outdoors will carry some risks. The challenge for free-range systems is to overcome the birds natural fear of wide-open spaces by providing cover in the environment to encourage more birds to go outdoors and venture away from the house. Smaller flocks, with smaller houses, are generally more successful at doing this. By choosing eggs carefully, you can help change the demand for a particular production system. Instead of the egg or the chicken it can be the egg and (good for) the chicken!

Dairy choices — not just black and white

Dr Jim Webster (PhD), Animal Behaviour and Welfare

Most dairy products in New Zealand are produced by cows. Cows are large, intelligent ruminants (i.e. they can digest grass and other plant matter). While they naturally live in social groups, with all the relationship interactions that can allow, they are generally quiet, peaceful animals. They graze for many hours a day, then will sit and relax to chew this material again (ruminate), which helps digest it further. They like shade (they easily get too hot in warm weather), and they dislike hard or muddy surfaces and standing for long periods.

To produce milk, a cow must first give birth to a calf and in New Zealand this is generally timed to happen in the spring so that lactation occurs while the grass is growing the best. Calves are generally removed from their mother shortly after birth and either reared separately or after four days sent away to be killed for human or pet food. Early separation of cow and calf is an unfortunate consequence of modern milk production that still needs to be solved by dairy industries worldwide.

The life of a cow that provides milk in New Zealand is typically pasture-based, which is beneficial for natural behaviour, rather than the indoor or lot-based systems found elsewhere in the world. Pasture-based dairy is not without challenges — such as feed quality, lack of shade, heat, cold and mud — but most can be solved by good management. Pasture-based dairy is the most common source for milk products in New Zealand supermarkets.

Unlike eggs, it is harder to choose milk from specific farms because of the mingling of milk from many farms in the tanker and at the factory. The availability of niche milk is increasing though, with single-farm sources and different milk types appearing. Goat milk and sheep milk are alternatives to cows. Dairy goats may live indoors and as usual it will pay to do some research on the milk available to you, to ensure it meets your expectations and matches your ethics.

Grow your own
Brooke Francis

Growing your own vegetables, fruits, herbs and sprouts has so many benefits — we could write a whole book on it. Not everyone has access to a big plot but even growing basil in a pot on your bench can be so satisfying.

Growing your own food is an easy way to monitor where your food comes from. We believe that home-grown veggies are some of the most nutritious you can get (we do love the farmers' market too, though). Preparing and cooking food with the seasonal vegetables coming from your garden is a rewarding way to get diversity into your diet (good for the gut microbiome, see page 48). We also think it helps improve consumption of fresh produce as we are probably more inclined to make an effort to eat what we grow — who wouldn't want to eat that bright red strawberry that you've been watching grow for a month?

Growing your own produce goes hand in hand with reducing plastic waste. It removes the need for packaging and for fruit and vegetables to be transported all over the country and globe. It can also be a good way to save money as the price for fresh produce has to account for all the transport miles and middle men. Learning to grow vegetables from seeds and saving your seeds from your own produce to grow the next year is another simple trick to save money on your grocery bill.

Healthy plants need healthy soil — just like we need fuelling, so does our garden. Shockingly, food scraps and cardboard do not break down in landfills as there is not enough oxygen, instead harmful gases are emitted as they begin to rot. No one should be putting food scraps in the bin! They are a precious resource that can be recycled and made into compost — a simple way of promoting a circular food economy.

Using a worm farm is a space-efficient way to compost food scraps. Along with their castings they also create 'worm wee' — both are great natural fertilisers to put on your garden. Just remember not to feed your worms onions, meat, oils, garlic or citrus — and help the little guys out by chopping scraps into small pieces.

A compost bin is also a simple solution for recycling fruit and vegetable scraps, provided you have the space for one. A compost bin needs a mix of 'green' and 'brown' matter. Green matter comes from plants and food scraps and brown matter comes from dead leaves, sticks and cardboard. A good compost heap requires a 50:50 ratio of these things and needs to be mixed regularly to aerate and dampen it so everything breaks down. You'll be surprised how quickly your old banana skins and egg shells break down into rich organic matter ready to fuel your plants and you.

One of the biggest benefits of a vegetable garden is for mental health. Gardening is a natural stress reliever and provides some wholesome time outside (often without your phone) to just relax and be one with nature. It is also satisfying and rewarding to watch and nurture plants into delicious fruits and vegetables that can be shared with friends and family. Whether you have a few pots or a large plot, give it a go!

Pantry staples
Brooke Francis

Apart from my shopping list, there are a few other things I like to consider when stocking my pantry.

Avoiding products that are packaged for single use is a simple way to cut down plastic waste. This can be done by filling jars at bulk bin stores, which generally sell everything from grains to spices to cleaning products. Avoiding plastic-packaged foods also helps avoid the possibility of BPA leaching into our food.

It is also important to shop locally to avoid creating food miles (carbon emissions from the transport of food) and to support local businesses. We should also vote with our money and choose to support companies whose values align with ours.

We have used a lot of canned legumes in our recipes. We recommend buying dried legumes such as chickpeas and lentils and soaking them, but we also understand that athletes are often tired, so reaching for a recyclable can is okay every now and then.

- Garlic and garlic crusher
- Brown onions
- Eggs
- Oats
- Ground cumin
- Paprika
- Ground turmeric
- Lentils
- Chickpeas
- Grains (rice, quinoa, etc.)
- Iodised salt
- Canned tomatoes
- Sesame seeds
- Pumpkin seeds
- Cold-pressed olive oil
- Raw apple cider vinegar
- Tahini
- Coconut milk and cream

Guest athletes

New Zealand athletes crushing it on the world stage and chasing conscious diets. Please note, opinions expressed are those of the athlete and not the authors.

Hugo Inglis — world-class Olympic hockey player

In New Zealand, we are blessed with countless opportunities to appreciate our natural environment. Growing up in the South Island I spent countless summers running around the coast, and winters in the mountains. This appreciation of our wild spaces was one of the major reasons I switched to a plant-based diet.

Our food system is completely broken and impacting the health and wellbeing of the climate, the ecology, the people, and the planet. Eating a plant-based diet gives us all the opportunity to reduce our footprint and incentivise [changing] the food system to one that can be reshaped to provide and nourish while enabling Papatūānuku to thrive.

Athletic performance was not my main reason for choosing a plant-based diet, yet after the change I was stronger, fitter, and faster. A well-balanced plant-based diet can be better for animals, the environment, and athletic performance.

Katie Cambie — accomplished multisport athlete

I love my vegetarian lifestyle. I have been fuelling myself that way for close to 20 years. Whilst maintaining my plant-based diet I train pretty hard so I can race long distances in my kayak down river. When I am not training

I manage New Zealand's biggest multisport kayak school, Topsport Kayaking. Our instructors teach people to kayak for the Kathmandu Coast to Coast Race. It is a very fast-paced active lifestyle so combine that with my own training and I need to make sure I am well fuelled. I paddle most days, along with running and biking. I have plenty of high-intensity intervals and workouts each week and a protein smoothie packed with nut butter, banana, dates, third-party tested protein and cocoa is my go-to post workout.

Brooke Neal — world-class Olympic hockey player

Brooke is an Olympian, and a former New Zealand hockey player, recently retiring after playing 176 games for the Black Sticks since her debut in 2014. She competed at the 2016 Olympic Games, and won gold at the Commonwealth Games in 2018. We asked her to share a bit about herself and her vegetarian journey.

Can you tell us a little about yourself?
Alongside my international hockey career, I am a mindset coach and founded All About Balance Ltd in 2016. During this time I have coached thousands of young female athletes to give them a greater sense of balance and wellbeing. I am also a registered yoga teacher, which I use to promote a healthy lifestyle and hauora.

How did you come to be a vegetarian?

I've been pescetarian for roughly four years, after trying to reduce my intake of any foods that can cause inflammation. I had four years of chronic pain in my knee (patellar tendinopathy), it's hard to know exactly what helped my healing since I was trying so many different things, but I managed to get pain free and so I stuck with the lifestyle of no meat. I loved the creativity and the flavours of vegetarian meals and it was relatively easy for me!

How did you find training and competing on a vegetarian diet?

I was expecting to notice a difference in my energy levels, as many people commented that my chosen lifestyle could affect my iron and B12 levels. But I felt really good and didn't notice a difference at all. If anything, I was waking up with more energy. It was difficult finding access to the right information, since there weren't many athletes at that stage that I knew who didn't eat meat. I had to be very wary of exactly what I was consuming each meal, and get blood tests to reassure me that I was tracking well.

What is your favourite meal?

I love them all; for breakfast, I mix some oats, blueberries, banana, flaxseed and honey for a delicious porridge with coconut yoghurt. For lunch, I generally have some combination of avocado, tomato, eggs or halloumi and greens. For dinner, I love making a bean mix that I can use in tacos, in a shepherd's pie, or for nachos. It's so versatile! But my favourite meal is home-made pizzas with mushrooms and eggplant.

Ruby Tui — professional rugby player, two-time Olympian, silver medallist Rio Olympics, gold medallist Tokyo Olympics

Can you tell us a little about yourself?

I am one of the first-ever professional female rugby players in New Zealand and I'm super grateful for that. Outside of the footy I love to research and learn about nutrition and mental health issues. I also love to just chill out with friends and family with some good music and good vibes. Playing for New Zealand has gotten me around the world a few times so I've been lucky to experience a few cultures and different foods. But when it comes to what food I eat, I call myself a conscious consumer.

What does it mean to be a conscious consumer?

I believe nutrition and the gut are directly linked to physical and mental health — what we fuel ourselves with impacts our performance and what we consciously decide to buy matters to our mentality in life. I'm not vegetarian or a vegan or anything; I'm not exclusively out of bounds to any particular food type, I just try to be conscious of what food I'm consuming. So when it comes to animal products, for example, I know there are animals that have been forced to breed and live in hideous conditions and there are farm practices that are not good for our planet — none of which I want to support. But there are also people who have a few animals that they care for dearly and they get older before they are used as a food source, which I don't have a problem with at all. I've also been in a situation of not [having] much money in a rural area where it was common to hunt wild animals for food, which I don't have a problem with eating. For me it's about being conscious of where my food has come from.

What are some of the key elements of nutrition that you focus on to be good at your sport?
Honestly, it's actually quite hard to be conscious at all times, especially when I'm on tour. Often when I ask where meats are sourced I get funny looks (even in Aotearoa). The obvious issue with not eating meat and dairy is the lack of protein within my diet but for years I have supplied my own protein powder outside of the team supply as non-dairy options were not funded when I first started. The last year or two has been a complete flip and now we always have lots of options, which is just awesome.

What aspects of food bring you joy?
Food that's fresh, and cooked with friends and family. Eating is a social activity when you're not on the go, and I think when you make the time to slow down to cook it well, and enjoy it, it makes it taste better too. I have also done a lot of travelling and I'm half Samoan so I love how culturally significant food is. In Samoa, food is an experience, a currency and always either freshly harvested or caught!

Do you have a go-to meal or recipe?
I make a smoothie that I have on the go all the time, using peanut butter, oats, banana, chia seeds, dates, almond and coconut milk.

Esther Keown — New Zealand runner, personal trainer and founder of Femmi

Can you tell us a little about yourself?
I am 29 years old and a happy human. I love life and am a very motivated person who loves the outdoors, animals, training and my family/friends. I have run for New Zealand in silver singlet events and won senior national medals in different distances. Running is definitely a big part of my life and I am really passionate about spreading the joy it brings to me with others. My mental health is a huge part of why I continue to run, it helps me feel rejuvenated, pumped for the day and inspired to get into other aspects of my life. I am passionate about women's health, inspiring young women to be the best versions of themselves, build confidence and embrace their bodies.

How did your diet come to be plant based? And how do you fuel yourself for training?
I am currently vegetarian as I eat all plant-based food as well as eggs. I became vege about three years ago now, I adore all animals and am really passionate about animal welfare as well as understanding I have a part to play in reducing the environmental impacts of certain

food production. It started with a feeling of guilt when I ate meat, contemplating if I needed it and if it was worth the pain inflicted on an innocent animal. I used to see the trucks filled with sheep and cows and burst into tears knowing I was part of their sad journey. I was inspired by some amazing athletes so started my journey with my partner. Since then, I have had to tailor my nutrition to be enough for an athlete; I have made sure that all aspects of my diet cover all bases required for a healthy functioning human and feel my body has responded so well to the change in diet. I feel proud that I am contributing to a better world with less pain for animals and reducing my impact on the environment.

We would love to hear about your coaching and your business . . .

I was lucky enough during the first lockdown (early 2020, when I lived in Sydney) to start a business called Femmi with my friends and fellow coaches Lydia O'Donnell and Paige Gilchrist.

Our goal is to inspire and educate women all over the world to understand and work with their bodies; we want to inspire all coaches, male and female, to understand female physiology and train their athletes accordingly. By teaching women that our menstrual cycle is something that we can use to our advantage, to better our performance and to use as a very obvious sign if something is not quite right within our bodies, we are hoping to change the way women see their body and embrace the way it functions in a holistic and healthy way.

What is your favourite meal?
My Crispy Cauli Mexican Tacos (see page 134).

Piera Hudson — New Zealand alpine ski racer

Can you tell us a little about yourself?
I am an alpine ski racer on the New Zealand Ski Team. I started skiing when I was four years old and started racing when I was eight. I have done 34 back-to-back winters representing New Zealand in Youth Olympics, World Junior Champs, World Champs, and on the Alpine World Cup tour, I am also a 10-time National Champion.

I grew up on a farm in Central Hawke's Bay and played every sport under the sun before finding my passion with skiing in the Southern Alps. When I was about 13 years old, I received a scholarship to attend a winter sports school academy in Vermont, USA, where we would fill our days with ski training, school work, and then gym training at night. I lived there for two years before moving over to Europe to start my professional career at age 15.

When I'm not skiing, I love spending time at the beach (working on my tan from the lack of summers) or in the gym for my training.

How did you come to be a vegetarian?
When I was about 19 I was given a book called *Eat & Run* by Scott Jurek, one of the most dominant ultramarathon runners in history. He talked about how going vegan was the best decision he ever made for his sporting career and how he owed his success to his diet change. I started to research more and more professional athletes from all sporting codes talking about how a plant-based diet gave them an edge over their competitors that they'd never had. How they were able to focus for longer, build muscle easier, and experience less inflammation and/or injuries.

I was intrigued as I was already mostly dairy-free but growing up on a sheep and beef farm my whole life, meat was all I'd known. I was travelling through Austria on a Sunday and the only thing open to get some food was the gas station. I picked up a dodgy-looking ham and cheese sandwich to eat on the go and, no surprise, spent that night on the bathroom floor with a severe case of food poisoning. I was flying home the next day (in a terrible state) and remember saying to myself, 'that's it, no more meat'. Unlike a lot of people who wisely wean themselves onto a more veggie diet, I went cold turkey from all animal-based products overnight.

It was hard at first and my parents, despite being supportive, definitely thought I was going to waste away as 'how could you ever get enough protein without eating meat?' But after a while, I figured out what worked for me and I could never go back!

How did you find training and competing on a vegetarian diet?
At first, I had no idea what I was doing and there was a lot of trial and error. I found it hardest when on the road competing in Europe or America as we often had to stay in hotels and I wasn't able to cook for myself. But in the last five years plant-based diets have seen exponential growth globally and I would say most people now have some idea of how to make a well-balanced vegan dish. I saw and felt immediate benefits when I initially went veggie and during my off-season, I was able to train harder and for longer and recover quicker in between sessions. I felt much more clear-headed and I rarely ever get bloated anymore. My metabolic age started reversing and I found it easier to lose fat and gain muscle during intense training blocks. I definitely don't miss that heavy feeling after eating meat or dairy.

What is your favourite meal?
I'm an absolute sucker for a Thai red or green tofu curry or my mum's loaded vegan nachos.

Ruby Tui

Esther Keown

Katie Cambie

Hugo Inglis

Recipes

Enjoy this mix of vegan and vegetarian recipes for breakfast, lunch, dinner, snacks, sides and desserts.

*Our recipes can easily be adapted for your dietary requirements — gluten-free and dairy-free alternatives work perfectly. Use your preferred choice throughout.

Brooke's Pancakes

VEGAN OPTION

I often have toast for my second breakfast (immediately after my first training session) but I love it when I have the time and energy to make myself pancakes!

Makes 6 pancakes

Pancakes
1¼ cups milk of
  your choice
2 tbsp maple syrup
1 medium banana
1½ cups flour of
  your choice
1 tbsp baking powder
¼ tsp baking soda
1 tsp ground cinnamon
  (optional)
Pinch of salt
Oil for cooking

Berry sauce
1½ cups frozen berries
1 tbsp lemon juice
1 tbsp water
1 tsp cornflour

For the pancakes, place all the ingredients in a food processor, starting with the wet ingredients first. Blitz to form a smooth, thick batter. Heat some oil in a skillet over a medium heat. Pour some batter on the skillet, roughly ⅓ cup per pancake. Leave to cook until bubbles appear on top, then flip gently. Cook for another 2–3 minutes until golden, then remove from the pan. Repeat with the remaining batter.

For the berry sauce, place the ingredients in a small pot over a medium heat and heat, stirring, until the berries have broken down and a thick sauce has formed.

Serve the pancakes with berry sauce or fresh berries and banana.

Tip: Athletes should have at least two pancakes. It is also recommended to add some protein to repair muscle damage caused by intense exercise – your choice of yoghurt will provide an extra protein hit.

	Per pancake	Per 100 g
Energy	204 kcal	126 kcal
Protein	6.4 g	3.9 g
Fat	1.8 g	1.1 g
Carbohydrate	28.8 g	23.9 g
Iron	0.8 mg	0.5 mg

Chia Pudding

Pudding for breakfast or lunch . . . yes, please.
Make this ahead and leave it overnight for
a quick breakfast before or after training.

Serves 1 athlete

1 cup milk
¼ cup chia seeds
2 tbsp desiccated coconut
1 tbsp maple syrup
½ tsp vanilla extract

To serve
Bananas
Blueberries
Walnuts
Honey
Coconut cream

Mix the ingredients in a bowl or mug. Cover and leave in the fridge for at least 2 hours.

Serve the chia pudding topped with bananas, blueberries, walnuts, honey and a dollop of coconut cream.

	Per serve	Per 100 g
Energy	611 kcal	109 kcal
Protein	20.7 g	3.7 g
Fat	27.1 g	4.9 g
Carbohydrate	64.0 g	11.5 g
Iron	3.9 mg	0.7 mg

Overnight Oats

A superb start to an action-packed day.

Serves 1 athlete

1 cup oats
½ cup blueberries
¼ cup walnuts
1 tsp ground cinnamon
2 tbsp chia seeds
1¼ cups milk

To serve
Drizzle of honey
Sliced banana

Place all the ingredients in a bowl. Mix well, cover and leave in the fridge overnight.

In the morning, serve topped with honey and banana.

	Per serve	Per 100 g
Energy	427.5 kcal	171 kcal
Protein	13.5 g	5.4 g
Fat	23.5 g	9.4 g
Carbohydrate	37.3 g	14.9 g
Iron	3.0 mg	1.2 mg

Brooke's Nana Pat's Muesli

Going to Nana Pat's house for home-made muesli is a favourite childhood memory. This is a great recipe to make with ingredients you can find at a bulk foods store and even better when you take your own containers to shop for them.

Makes about 10 serves

3 cups rolled oats
1 cup wheat bran
½ cup seeds (we
    use pumpkin)
½ cup nuts (we
    use cashews)
¼ cup desiccated coconut
¼ cup vegetable oil
2 tbsp honey
2 tbsp brown sugar
¼ cup dried fruit (we
    use apricots)

Preheat the oven to 200°C.

Place the rolled oats, wheat bran, seeds, nuts and coconut in a large baking dish, mix well to combine then spread out into a even layer.

Bake in the oven for around 20 minutes or until the mixture starts to crisp and is slightly golden.

Meanwhile, place the oil, honey and brown sugar in a small pot and heat for 5-10 minutes over a low heat until combined.

Remove the dry ingredients from the oven and turn off the heat.

Pour the wet ingredients over the dry ingredients, mix well and spread out into an even layer.

Return to the the still-warm oven for 20 minutes, then remove and set aside to cool.

When cold, add any dried fruit you like and store in an airtight container for up to 2 weeks.

Serve with milk or yoghurt and extra fruit, if desired.

	Per serve	Per 100 g
Energy	284 kcal	436 kcal
Protein	7.7 g	12.2 g
Fat	15.8 g	24.2 g
Carbohydrate	24.4 g	37.5 g
Iron	2.8 mg	4.3 mg

Smoothies

Make before training and consume straight after to get the necessary protein and carbohydrates for recovery.

Energiser Smoothie

VEGAN

Serves 1 athlete

¾ cup fresh pineapple (or canned)
¾ cup frozen or fresh mango
2 tbsp chia seeds
1 tsp ground turmeric
1 tsp peeled and grated ginger
¼ cup water

Place all the ingredients in a blender and blend until smooth, adding more water if the consistency is too thick.

	Per serve	Per 100 g
Energy	167.5 kcal	67 kcal
Protein	3.0 g	1.2 g
Fat	0.5 g	0.2 g
Carbohydrate	25.5 g	10.2 g
Iron	2.0 mg	0.8 mg

Kate Cambie's Peanut Butter Smoothie

Serves 1 athlete

1 frozen banana, peeled
½ cup peanut butter
1½ cups milk
1 tbsp cocoa
4 dates
2 heaped tbsp protein powder

Place all the ingredients in a blender and blend until smooth, adding more water if the consistency is too thick.

	Per serve	Per 100 g
Energy	507.5 kcal	203 kcal
Protein	18.8 g	7.5 g
Fat	35.0 g	14.0 g
Carbohydrate	29 g	11.6 g
Iron	1.25 mg	0.5 mg

Green Smoothie

VEGAN

Serves 1 athlete

1 avocado, peeled
1 frozen banana, peeled
1 kiwifruit, peeled
1 cup spinach
½ cup water

Place all the ingredients in a blender and
blend until smooth, adding more water if the
consistency is too thick.

	Per serve	Per 100 g
Energy	180 kcal	72 kcal
Protein	3.0 g	1.2 g
Fat	10.8 g	4.3 g
Carbohydrate	14.0 g	5.6 g
Iron	1.0 mg	0.4 mg

Savoury French Toast

Sick of eggs on toast. French toast is a simple and delicious variation.

Serves 1 athlete

Pickled onion
¼ cup white wine vinegar
1 tbsp white sugar
1 tsp salt
1 red onion, sliced

French toast
2 free-range eggs
½ cup grated cheese
  (Edam or Parmesan)
2 tbsp milk
Salt and pepper
1 tbsp butter
2 or 3 thick slices of
  sourdough (or whatever
  bread you have)

To serve (optional)
Kimchi
Spinach
Tomatoes or tomato
  chutney
Basil
Matcha latte

For the pickled onion, place the vinegar, sugar and salt in a bowl and stir to dissolve the sugar. Add the onion and a little water if needed to cover the onion. Leave to sit until you've finished making the French toast.

For the French toast, place the eggs, cheese, milk, salt and pepper in a bowl and whisk together. Melt the butter in a skillet set over a medium heat. Dip slices of bread into the egg mixture, then place them in the skillet. Cook for 3-5 minutes on both sides or until golden and crispy.

Serve the French toast with pickled onion, kimchi, spinach, tomatoes or a tomato chutney, basil and a matcha latte on the side.

	Per serve	Per 100 g
Energy	762 kcal	236 kcal
Protein	40.9 g	12.7 g
Fat	41.2 g	12.8 g
Carbohydrate	54.1 g	16.8 g
Iron	3.5 mg	1.1 mg

Egg Breakfast Wraps

This is a great dish for a protein and carb hit post-training and is also an easy alternative to mundane toast or porridge.

Serves 1

2 free-range eggs
Salt and pepper
½ cup sliced mushrooms
1 tbsp butter or oil
1 spring onion, sliced
1 small bunch parsley,
    finely chopped
1 handful of baby spinach,
    finely chopped
2 wholemeal tortillas
Tomato paste or
    tomato relish
Oil for cooking
1 tomato, diced
⅓ cup grated cheese
    (optional)

Place the eggs in a bowl and beat together with some salt and pepper. Set aside. Place the mushrooms in a pan with butter or oil and cook for a few minutes until browned. Set aside. Place the greens in a bowl and mix together. Set aside. Coat one side of each wrap with the tomato paste or relish.

Heat a medium-sized frying pan (preferably the same size as the wraps or a little bigger) over a medium heat. Add a little oil to cover the bottom of the pan. Add half of the egg and move the pan around until the bottom of the pan is evenly covered with a thin layer of egg. Cook for 30 seconds and then place the tortilla, tomato paste side down, on top of the egg mixture. Cook for a further 30 seconds, then flip the whole thing over to brown the other side of the wrap. Transfer to a plate. Add the mushrooms, greens, diced tomato and cheese, if using, and roll up. Repeat with the next tortilla and egg mixture.

Serve immediately.

	Per serve	Per 100 g
Energy	640 kcal	121 kcal
Protein	33.1 g	6.3 g
Fat	29.1 g	5.5 g
Carbohydrate	57.1 g	10.8 g
Iron	5.0 mg	0.9 mg

Baked Beans with Yoghurt and Oat Flatbread

This meal is excellent in everything: carbohydrate, protein and taste. You can also eat the flatbread as a snack, topped with hummus, or they make an easy pizza base!

Serves 2 athletes

Beans

1 tbsp olive oil
1 brown onion,
  finely chopped
2 tsp minced garlic
½ tsp ground cumin
1½ tsp smoked paprika
1¾ cups Tomato Passata
  (see page 109) or 400 g
  can crushed tomatoes
1½ cups cooked
  cannellini or borlotti
  beans or 400 g can
½ tsp Marmite
Salt and pepper

Flatbread

1 cup oat flour (blend
  oats to a powder) or
  regular wholemeal flour,
  plus extra for dusting
½ cup plain yoghurt
1 tsp baking powder
½ tsp salt
Pepper (optional)

To make the baked beans, heat the olive oil in a frying pan set over a low-medium heat. Add the onion to the pan and sauté for 3 minutes. Add the garlic and cook for a further 2 minutes. Add the cumin and paprika and cook for 1 minute. Add the remainder of the baked beans ingredients and simmer for 20 minutes until the sauce is thick.

While the beans simmer, make the flatbread.

Mix the ingredients together in a large bowl. Divide the mixture into 2-4 pieces, depending on how large you want your flatbreads. Dust a work surface with flour and roll each piece out until about 0.5 cm thick. Heat a frying pan to a medium temperature and add a little oil. Cook each piece of bread for 2-3 minutes on each side or until nicely browned.

	1 large flatbread	Per 100 g
Energy	571 kcal	208 kcal
Protein	24.4 g	8.9 g
Fat	8.4 g	3.1 g
Carbohydrate	89.2 g	32.5 g
Iron	4.4 mg	1.6 mg

	Per serve of beans	Per 100 g
Energy	766 kcal	157 kcal
Protein	42.9 g	8.8 g
Fat	15.0 g	3.1 g
Carbohydrate	80.3 g	16.5 g
Iron	18.5 mg	3.8 mg

Corn Fritters
VEGAN OPTION

These are perfect for breakfast, lunch or dinner!

Serves 2 athletes

¾ cup flour of your choice
½ tsp baking powder
½ tsp salt
Cracked black
  pepper, to taste
½ cup milk of your choice
1 cup corn (fresh off the
  cob, canned or frozen)
½ red capsicum or red
  onion, chopped
2 spring onions, sliced
Oil for cooking

To serve
Sour cream
Extra sliced spring onions

Place the flour, baking powder, salt and pepper in a large bowl. Add the milk and whisk to combine. The batter should be thick, if it looks too dry add a little more milk. Fold in the corn, capsicum and spring onions.

Heat a large skillet over a medium heat then drizzle in a little oil to coat the pan. Use a ¼ cup measure to scoop batter out of the bowl and into the pan. As they cook, gently flatten each fritter with a spatula. Repeat with remaining batter. You might have to do it in 2 batches to avoid overcrowding the pan. Cook the fritters for 3-4 minutes on each side or until golden brown. Top with sour cream and sliced spring onions.

Tip: To increase the protein of this meal you could add an egg or a green salad with seeds and nuts.

	Per serve	Per 100 g
Energy	446 kcal	130 kcal
Protein	12.8 g	3.7 g
Fat	12.7 g	3.9 g
Carbohydrate	67.0 g	19.4 g
Iron	1.5 mg	0.4 mg

Pickled Eggs on Toast

The flavour of these pickled eggs really adds an extra dimension to eggs on toast. Make them ahead of time and just pull them out of the fridge for a quick and tasty meal or snack.

Serves 3 athletes

6 free-range eggs
½ cup water
1 cup apple cider vinegar
2 tsp ground turmeric
1 tsp sugar
½ onion, thinly sliced
1 tsp salt
2 cloves garlic, sliced

To serve
6 slices of rye bread (or
  any bread you prefer)
Butter (to spread
  on your toast)

Bring a pot of water to the boil. Using a ladle, lower the eggs into the boiling water and boil for 7-8 minutes. Meanwhile, in another pot, heat the water and apple cider vinegar to a warm temperature. Add the turmeric, sugar, onion, salt and garlic and stir to combine. Remove from the heat. Drain the cooked eggs and rinse under cold water until cold enough to peel. Place the peeled eggs and the vinegar mixture in a jar or container. Refrigerate for at least 1 hour before eating. The eggs will keep in the vinegar solution for up to 6 days in the fridge.

To serve, slice 2 eggs thinly and layer on top of your toast.

Tip: This is a fantastic meal before or after your training session. You could add a tomato or a piece of fruit to make it a complete meal.

	Per serve	Per 100 g
Energy	476 kcal	140 kcal
Protein	21.6 g	6.3 g
Fat	17.5 g	5.1 g
Carbohydrate	50.7 g	14.8 g
Iron	3.9 mg	1.2 mg

Shakshuka with Beans

This is a yum meal to share with friends.

Serves 4 athletes

Oil for cooking
1 brown onion, diced
1 red capsicum,
  deseeded and diced
4 cloves garlic,
  finely chopped
2 tsp paprika
1 tsp ground cumin
1 tsp ground coriander
¼ tsp chilli powder
2 x 400 g cans
  chopped tomatoes
400 g can borlotti or
  cannellini beans
Salt and pepper
6 free-range eggs
Coriander, to garnish

Heat some oil in a frying pan over a medium heat. Add the onion and capsicum and sauté for a few minutes until the onion is translucent. Add the garlic and spices and cook for another minute. Mix in the tomatoes and beans, add salt and pepper to taste, and bring to a simmer. Make a well in the mixture with a large spoon and crack in an egg. Repeat for the remaining eggs. Cover with a lid and cook until the eggs are done. Garnish with coriander.

Tip: Top this dish up with chopped feta and serve with wholemeal toast for a complete meal.

	Per serve	Per 100 g
Energy	282 kcal	59 kcal
Protein	18.2 g	3.8 g
Fat	7.2 g	1.5 g
Carbohydrate	34.3 g	7.1 g
Iron	5.9 mg	1.2 mg

Sprouts
VEGAN

They may be small, but sprouts pack a powerful nutritional punch.

Your choice of
2 tbsp mung beans
3 tbsp alfalfa seeds
2 tbsp broccoli seeds
2 tbsp whole lentils

You will need
1 large sterilised
  jar (mason jar)
1 square muslin cloth
  or fine mesh
1 rubber band

Add your selected beans, seeds or lentils to the jar, put the muslin cloth on top of the jar and secure with the rubber band. Add water and rinse. Do this 3-4 times. After rinsing, add enough water to cover the contents and leave to soak overnight. After about 12 hours, drain the water and rinse them again. Leave the drained jar in a cool dark area. Continue to rinse the contents at least twice a day for the next 2-3 days. After 2-3 days you should notice them sprout. Leave them on a bench in sunlight for 1 day to turn green, continuing to rinse twice a day.

Your sprouts should be ready now. Store them in the fridge in an airtight container and use within the next 5 days.

Note: Sulforaphane is a sulphur-rich compound found in green vegetables. It is especially abundant in broccoli sprouts. Sulforaphane is a powerful phytochemical that can neutralise toxins in our body by cancelling free radicals, which are tiny particles that weaken and damage the healthy cells in our bodies. This process also reduces inflammation in our bodies and may protect our DNA by blocking mutations that can lead to cancer.

Eggless Aioli

VEGAN

We always save the brine from canned chickpeas to make this easy eggless aioli. To make mayonnaise, just leave out the garlic.

Makes 1½ cups

3 tbsp aquafaba
2 tbsp apple cider vinegar or lemon juice
½ tsp Dijon mustard
1 cup vegetable oil
2–3 cloves garlic
Salt and pepper to taste

Place all the ingredients in a tall jug and whizz with a stick blender for about 1 minute until thick and creamy. Store in an airtight container in the fridge for up to 2 weeks.

Basil and Walnut Pesto

VEGAN

This is a cheap and tasty alternative to pine nut pesto. Serve on toast with tomato and mozzarella or mix through pasta for a quick and easy lunch or dinner.

Makes 1 cup

1–2 large handfuls of basil
½ cup walnuts
2 tbsp nutritional yeast
2 tbsp lemon juice
2 tsp minced garlic
Drizzle of olive oil
Salt and pepper

Place all the ingredients in a food processor and pulse until combined. Add water if the mixture is too thick and pulse until you have a smooth pesto.

Store in a glass container in the fridge for up to 5 days or freeze in an ice cube tray to use later.

Hummus

Hummus is the best hangry snack! Full of protein, it will hit the hunger cravings and keep you feeling full. Serve it with crackers or kūmara (pan-fried or baked in the oven).

Easy Chickpea Hummus

VEGAN

Makes 2 cups

400 g can chickpeas, drained
2 tbsp tahini
2 tbsp lemon juice
2 tsp minced garlic
1 tsp ground cumin
¼ tsp cayenne pepper
½ cup water or as required

Place the chickpeas, tahini, lemon juice, garlic, cumin and cayenne pepper in a food processor and blitz until combined. Add water if needed to get it to the consistency you want.

Beetroot Butter Bean Hummus

VEGAN

Makes 2 cups

400 g can butter beans
1 large roasted beetroot, cooled, peeled and diced
2 tbsp lemon juice
1 tbsp olive oil
1 tsp minced garlic
Salt and pepper
½ cup water or as required

Place the butter beans, beetroot, lemon juice, olive oil, garlic, salt and pepper in a food processor and blitz until combined. Add water if needed to get it to the consistency you want.

Tomato Passata

VEGAN

What do you do when your tomato plant is exploding with tomatoes? You make passata! We love using this sauce with pasta or mixing it with beans and seasoning to make Mexican beans.

Makes 800 ml

1 tbsp olive oil
1 brown onion, diced
6 whole cloves
    garlic, peeled
1 kg tomatoes, halved or
    quartered, depending
    on their size
Handful of basil
Salt and pepper
1 tsp caster sugar

Heat the olive oil in a pot set over a medium heat. Add the onion and garlic and fry for a few minutes until translucent. Add the tomatoes and basil, then cover and cook for 10 minutes, stirring occasionally, until the tomatoes have collapsed. Season with salt and pepper and add the sugar. Remove the lid and boil for 10 minutes until the garlic is soft.

Allow the mixture to cool and then blend to remove the lumps. If you don't have a blender, you can use a sieve to remove the large bits from the mixture.

Pour into jars and keep in the fridge for up to a week, or put into containers and freeze for later use.

To make this into a thick pizza sauce, heat a large frying pan over a medium heat. Add 2 cups of tomato passata and add some dried herb seasoning for flavour. Cook for 5-7 minutes until the sauce has reduced.

Saucy tip: When growing your own tomatoes, plant them next to basil as the two grow well together as companion plants. Remember to give your plants lots of water for juicer tomatoes.

Tofu Noodle Soup

VEGAN

This is a super-easy, flavoursome, one-pot meal with the added bonus of being good for the gut.

Serves 4 athletes

Oil for cooking
1 brown onion, diced
2 tsp minced garlic
1 tsp minced ginger
1 tsp minced chilli
3–4 tbsp miso paste
2 tsp vegetable
  stock powder
6 cups hot water
2 cups shelled
  edamame beans
300 g tofu, diced
250 g quinoa rice noodles
  or soba noodles
1 bunch spring
  onions, sliced
1 nori sheet, cut into
  slivers (optional)

To serve (optional)
Fried shallots

Heat some oil in a big pot. Add the onion, garlic, ginger and chilli and fry until the onion is golden. Add the miso paste, stock powder and hot water and heat, but don't boil, until the miso paste has dissolved. Add the edamame beans, tofu and noodles and heat for 10-20 minutes until the noodles are cooked through. Add the spring onion and nori, if using, during the final minutes of cooking.

Serve the soup with fried shallots sprinkled on top, if desired.

Tip: This makes an excellent recovery meal as it contains sufficient amounts of carbohydrate and protein as well as fluids.

	Per serve	Per 100 g
Energy	545 kcal	320 kcal
Protein	33 g	4.6 g
Fat	17.4 g	2.4 g
Carbohydrate	63.0 g	8.8 g
Iron	6.5 mg	0.9 mg

Super Orange Soup

VEGAN

This yummy vegan soup can be made in a slow cooker or on the stove top.

Serves 2–3 athletes

1 brown onion, diced
2 cloves garlic,
  finely chopped
1 tbsp ground turmeric
2–3 cm piece
  ginger, grated
3 cups water
2 cups vegetable stock
⅓ cup orange juice
1 cup red lentils
1 orange kūmara,
  peeled and diced
1 small butternut
  squash, diced (approx.
  500 g when peeled
  and deseeded)
Salt and pepper

Slow cooker:
Place all the ingredients in a slow cooker and mix well with a spoon. Cook on low for 6 hours or on high for 4 hours.

Stovetop:
Heat some oil in a large pot over a medium heat. Add the onion and garlic and lightly fry until the onion is translucent. Add the turmeric and ginger, cook for a further minute, then add all the remaining ingredients. Bring to the boil, then reduce the heat to low. Simmer, covered, for 1 hour, or until the vegetables are cooked. Season to taste.

Once cooked, mash the vegetables or blend the soup to your desired consistency.

Tip: Add feta and/or toasted pumpkin seeds to increase the protein content of this meal. Serve it with Yoghurt and Oat Flatbread (see page 94) to increase the carbohydrates. You could also top the soup with some crispy kale for extra flavour.

	Per serve	Per 100 g
Energy	83 kcal	33 kcal
Protein	3.5 g	1.4 g
Fat	0.5 g	0.2 g
Carbohydrate	13.5 g	5.4 g
Iron	1.5 mg	0.6 mg

James Coote's Broccoli and Blue Cheese Soup

Brooke's coach James is a fantastic chef and has created this divine recipe. Athletes will need to add some extra protein and carbohydrate (e.g. bread) or it could work as a delicious starter before a main dish. Match this dish with a glass of Pinot Noir.

Serves 4 coaches

3–4 large broccoli
  heads, florets cut off
  (use the stalks for
  something else, they're
  too woody for soup)
3 cups vegetable stock
Salt and pepper
125 g blue cheese
  (I use Kāpiti Cheese
  Kikorangi Blue)
2 tbsp mayonnaise

To serve
Crusty bread
Olive oil

Place the broccoli florets in a pot with the stock and seasonings and gently bring to the boil. Cook for 5-7 minutes until the broccoli is soft. Ladle the soup into a blender while still hot and pulse to break up. Add the whole piece of cheese and mayonnaise to the blender and blend until the soup is super smooth and thick. If it's too thick, add some more stock or white wine or water. Season with salt and pepper to taste.

Serve with some crusty bread and a drizzle of olive oil on top.

Training match: 3 x 20-minute up-downs on a rowing machine.

	Per serve	Per 100 g
Energy	261 kcal	54 kcal
Protein	18.8 g	3.9 g
Fat	17.2 g	3.5 g
Carbohydrate	2.7 g	0.5 g
Iron	2.3 mg	0.5 mg

Zucchini Slice

This is a great summer recipe for using up all those zucchini in the garden.

Makes 12 squares

2 cups spinach leaves

5 free-range eggs

1 cup self-raising
  flour, sifted

4 large zucchini, grated

1 large onion, finely
  chopped

100 g feta

¼ cup olive oil

⅓ cup sun-dried
  tomatoes (optional)

½ cup pumpkin seeds

Preheat the oven to 170ºC bake. Grease and line a 30 cm x 20 cm pan or similarly sized baking dish.

Wilt the spinach in a dry pan over a low heat until soft. Remove and allow to cool before squeezing out any excess liquid. Place the eggs in a large bowl and beat well. Add the flour and beat until smooth, then add the spinach, zucchini, onion, feta, olive oil and sun-dried tomatoes, if using. Stir to combine. Pour the mixture into the prepared dish and top with the pumpkin seeds. Bake for 30 minutes until cooked through. Slice into 12 squares and store in the fridge.

Tip: Eat as part of a lunch with bread and green salad with extra feta and loads of seeds and nuts to increase both carbohydrate and protein.

	Per serve	Per 100 g
Energy	189 kcal	175 kcal
Protein	8.6 g	8.0 g
Fat	11.9 g	11.0 g
Carbohydrate	11.1 g	10.3 g
Iron	1.7 mg	1.5 mg

Beetroot, Feta and Brown Rice Salad

This is a yum post-training meal to recover from those intense training sessions; it's high in carbohydrates and provides sufficient protein to speed up recovery and help repair your muscles. It's also a great dish to take to potluck dinners.

Serves 4 athletes

2 cups brown rice
⅓ cup olive oil
1 small red onion, diced
1 tsp ground cumin
1 tsp ground coriander
2 cups roasted
  beetroot, cubed
400 g can chickpeas or
  350 g cooked chickpeas
1 cup mint leaves,
  roughly chopped
200 g baby spinach or kale
½ cup toasted walnuts,
  coarsely chopped
3 tbsp balsamic vinegar
200 g feta, crumbled

Cook the rice in a large pot of salted, boiling water for 20 minutes, then drain. Meanwhile, heat 1 tablespoon of the oil in a large frying pan over a medium heat. Add the onion and cook, stirring, for 5 minutes or until softened. Add the cumin and coriander and cook, stirring, for 30 seconds. Add the beetroot and chickpeas and stir until everything is heated through.

In a salad bowl, combine the cooled rice, mint, spinach, walnuts and drizzle with 2 tablespoons of the balsamic vinegar and the remaining 2 tablespoons of olive oil. Add the beetroot and chickpea mixture and toss together. Crumble over the feta and drizzle with the remaining tablespoon of balsamic vinegar.

	Per serve	Per 100 g
Energy	919 kcal	233 kcal
Protein	24.2 g	6.1 g
Fat	49.1 g	12.4 g
Carbohydrate	89.4 g	22.7 g
Iron	4.5 mg	1.1 mg

Jacket Potatoes

Who doesn't love potatoes?

Serves 4 athletes

Mexican seasoning
1 tsp each: ground cumin,
  ground coriander,
  smoked paprika
½ tsp each: chilli powder,
  onion powder, garlic salt

Potatoes
4 large baking potatoes
Olive oil, for coating

Mexican beans
1 tbsp olive oil
1 onion, finely chopped
1 capsicum, finely
  chopped
400 g can black beans
¼ cup Tomato Passata
  (see page 109)
  or ¼ cup canned
  crushed tomatoes
¼ cup water

To serve
¾ cup grated cheese
1 large handful of
  spinach leaves
½ yellow capsicum, diced
1 tomato, chopped
1 avocado, peeled
  and chopped

Preheat the oven to 180°C.

For the Mexican seasoning, mix all the ingredients together.
Set aside until required.

For the potatoes, put them in a microwave-proof dish and
microwave on high for 8 minutes, then place on an oven tray,
lightly coat with olive oil and bake for 1 hour.

For the Mexican beans, heat the olive oil in a pot over a
medium heat. Add the onion and capsicum and cook for a
few minutes to soften. Add the beans, passata, water and
Mexican seasoning and cook for 10 minutes.

To serve, remove the baked potatoes from the oven and switch
to the grill function. Allow the potatoes to cool slightly, then
cut a cross on the top of each and squeeze them open. Top
each potato with the Mexican beans and then cheese. Brown
under the grill for 5 minutes

Serve on a bed of spinach leaves and yellow capsicum with
tomato and avocado on the side.

	Per serve	Per 100 g
Energy	441 kcal	84 kcal
Protein	21.6 g	41 g
Fat	17.1 g	3.3 g
Carbohydrate	39.4 g	7.5 g
Iron	4.1 mg	0.8 mg

Pumpkin and Feta Filo Log

Roast pumpkin and filo — such a scrumptious combination!

Serves 3 athletes

400 g pumpkin, peeled and
   diced into 2 cm cubes
1 red onion, sliced
1 tbsp olive oil
Salt and pepper
1 tbsp curry powder
1 cup well-packed
   spinach leaves
⅓ cup chopped
   dates or raisins
100 g feta
⅓ cup chopped parsley

To serve
Natural yoghurt
Green salad

Preheat the oven to 180°C.

Put the pumpkin and onion in a roasting dish, coat with the olive oil and season with salt and pepper. Bake for 30 minutes until soft. Remove from the oven and sprinkle with the curry powder. Add the spinach and mix in so that it wilts. Leave to cool for about 5 minutes. Add the dates or raisins, feta and parsley and roughly mix.

To assemble the filo log, place a stack of 5 sheets of filo pastry on a large chopping board or clean bench top. Add the mixture in a log shape along the middle of the pastry. Leave about 4 cm at each end. You want a good amount of filling, but be mindful that you don't overfill. Pick up the edge of the pastry sheet closest to you and fold over the top of the mixture. Tuck in the sides, and continue to roll until it resembles a huge spring roll. Place on a flat baking tray and bake until the pastry is golden, about 10 minutes. Remove from the oven and cut into three.

Serve with natural yoghurt and a green salad.

	Per serve	Per 100 g
Energy	2773 kcal	103 kcal
Protein	10.5 g	4.0 g
Fat	14.4 g	5.4 g
Carbohydrate	23.4 g	8.8 g
Iron	2.5 mg	1.0 mg

Asian Noodle Salad

This salad is our go-to for summer barbecues or potlucks. All our friends love it, and it means we vegetarians have a well-rounded meal when there is not a lot else for us on offer.

Serves 4 athletes

¼ cup sesame seeds
¼ cup pumpkin seeds
½ cup peanuts
200 g block halloumi, diced
250 g noodles (we use
  quinoa rice noodles)

Sauce

2 tbsp peanut butter
2 tbsp sesame oil
2 tbsp olive oil
1 tbsp soy sauce
1 tsp minced chilli
1 tsp minced garlic

Salad

¼ red or green
  cabbage, shredded
2 carrots, julienned
  (peeled first if desired)
½ red capsicum, sliced
2–3 spring onions, sliced

Toast the sesame seeds and pumpkin seeds in a dry frying pan. Combine with the peanuts and set aside.

In the same pan, fry the halloumi until brown on each side and set aside.

Boil the noodles in a large pot of water over a medium heat until al dente. Drain and set aside.

For the sauce, place all the ingredients in a pot over a medium heat, stirring to combine. Add a little water if the mixture becomes too thick.

To assemble the salad, place all the vegetables in a large serving bowl. Add the halloumi, noodles and sauce and mix well to combine.

Serve the salad topped with the peanut mixture.

Tip: Endurance athletes could add some extra bread to increase the carbohydrate component of their meal.

	Per serve	Per 100 g
Energy	753 kcal	276 kcal
Protein	28.9 g	10.6 g
Fat	57.9 g	21.2 g
Carbohydrate	27.0 g	9.9 g
Iron	3.5 mg	1.3 mg

Plant Nachos

VEGAN

There are 101 different ways to make nachos, so we thought we would offer this spiced-up option, which contains a great amount of carbs and protein for athletes.

Serves 4 athletes

Refried beans
1 tbsp olive oil
1 brown onion, diced
8 mushrooms, sliced
2 tbsp minced garlic
400 g can butter
  beans, drained
400 g can black
  beans, drained
2 tsp ground cumin
1 tsp dried oregano

Cheesy sauce
1 cup peeled and
  diced potato
1 cup cashews
1 cup unsweetened
  dairy-free milk
3 tbsp nutritional yeast
3 tbsp apple cider vinegar
1 tsp salt
1 tsp minced garlic

To serve
Corn chips or cooked rice

Toppings (your choice of)
½ cup sliced olives
2 handfuls of baby spinach
1 tomato, diced
¼ cup sliced jalapeños
½ red capsicum, diced

For the refried beans, heat the oil in a medium frying pan. Add the onion, mushrooms and garlic and sauté over a medium heat for a few minutes. Add the butter beans, black beans, cumin and oregano and continue to cook until the beans are soft. Once soft, remove from the heat and mash with a fork until smooth. You may need to add some boiling water to get the consistency you desire.

For the cheesy sauce, cook the potato and cashews in a pot of boiling water over a medium heat for about 10 minutes or until soft. Remove from the heat and drain well. Place the potato and cashews in a food processor or blender with the milk, nutritional yeast, apple cider vinegar, salt and garlic and blend until smooth.

Serve the refried beans over corn chips or rice. Add the toppings of your choice and finish with the cheesy sauce.

	Per serve	Per 100 g
Energy	863 kcal	132 kcal
Protein	35.0 g	5.4 g
Fat	39.2 g	6.0 g
Carbohydrate	81.9 g	12.5 g
Iron	12.5 mg	1.9 mg

Broccoli and Mushroom Filo Log

This yummy filo log is made with broccoli and mushroom, but as this dish is quite low on carbohydrates you could replace them with starchy carbohydrates (e.g. pumpkin and/or potato) if you're using this as a recovery meal.

Serves 3 athletes

1 tablespoon oil
1 head of broccoli,
  finely chopped
1 cup finely chopped
  mushrooms
2 cloves garlic,
  finely chopped
1 cup well-packed
  spinach leaves
½ cup chopped parsley
½ cup tasty or feta cheese
5 sheets filo pastry
¼ cup butter, melted

To serve
Natural yoghurt
Green salad

Preheat the oven to 180°C.

Heat the oil in a medium frying pan over a medium heat. Add the broccoli and sauté for about 4 minutes. Add the mushrooms and garlic and sauté for another few minutes until the mushroom is cooked. Remove from the heat and add the spinach and parsley. Let the mixture cool for 5 minutes before mixing in the cheese.

To assemble the filo log, place a stack of 5 sheets of filo pastry on a large chopping board or clean bench top. Brush melted butter between each layer. Add the mixture in a log shape along the middle of the pastry. Leave about 4 cm at each end. You want a good amount of filling, but be mindful that you don't overfill.

Pick up the edge of the pastry sheets closest to you and fold over the top of the mixture. Tuck in the sides, and continue to roll until it resembles a huge spring roll. Place on a flat baking tray and bake until the pastry is golden, about 10 minutes. Remove from the oven and cut into three.

Serve with natural yoghurt and a green salad.

Tip: Top up this dish with protein and carbohydrates to make it a complete meal for athletes.

	Per serve	Per 100 g
Energy	214 kcal	89 kcal
Protein	13.3 g	5.6 g
Fat	8.0 g	3.4 g
Carbohydrate	18.2 g	7.6 g
Iron	2.6 mg	1.1 mg

Home-made Wraps with Falafel and Greek Yoghurt Dressing

Makes 8 wraps

Wraps
6 free-range eggs
2 tbsp olive oil
1 tsp cornflour
Salt and pepper
Oil for frying

Falafel
400 g can chickpeas, drained
2 tsp minced garlic
1 tsp ground cumin
1 tsp dried oregano
3 tbsp flour
Salt and pepper
Oil for frying

Greek yoghurt dressing
½ cup Greek yoghurt
2 tbsp lemon juice
1 tbsp olive oil
1 tsp dried oregano
Salt and pepper

Making these gluten-free wraps is more time-consuming than using store-bought ones but they are honestly so good. They don't fall apart or crack, and they are packed with protein. This filling goes well with any salad items or our Avo Slaw (see page 147).

For the wraps, place all the ingredients in a bowl and beat with an eggbeater or whisk until smooth. Heat a frying pan and coat with the oil. Pour ¼ cup of the mixture into the frying pan and spread to make a big circle. Cook for about a minute on each side. Set aside and do the same with the remaining mixture to make 8 wraps in total.

For the falafel, place all the ingredients except the oil into a food processor and blitz unti smooth. You may need to add more water or flour, depending on whether the mixture is too dry or too wet. Form the mixture into 8 patties. Heat some oil in a frying pan and fry the falafel patties until golden, about 4 minutes on each side.

For the dressing, mix all the ingredients together in a bowl.

Serve the wraps filled with falafel and dressing with a salad or avo slaw on the side.

Tip: Athletes with a high energy expenditure should make sure that they have at least 2 or 3 wraps to ensure that they are consuming sufficient carbohydrates and protein.

	Per wrap	Per 100 g
Energy	210 kcal	703 kcal
Protein	9.8 g	7.8 g
Fat	12.5 g	10.0 g
Carbohydrate	12.3 g	9.9 g
Iron	2.6 mg	2.1 mg

Potato and Spinach Frittata

Eggs are so versatile! Here's a protein-packed method that's bound to satisfy as well as tantalise the tastebuds.

Serves 4 athletes

Oil for cooking
6 small potatoes,
  peeled and diced
  into 2 cm chunks
½ cup water
½ cup chopped
  mushrooms
2 cloves garlic, minced
1 tsp smoked paprika
1 cup well-packed spinach
  leaves or frozen spinach
8 free-range eggs
¼ cup milk
1 tbsp flour
Handful of parsley,
  chopped
Salt and pepper
100 g feta
⅓ cup pumpkin seeds

Preheat the oven to 180°C. Oil the sides and bottom of a 25 cm x 15 cm baking dish.

Heat some oil in a large skillet over a medium heat. Add the potatoes and water, cover and cook for 10 minutes until the potatoes are soft. Pour out any excess water and return the skillet to the hob. Add the mushrooms and cook for 2 minutes. Add the garlic, smoked paprika and spinach and continue to cook until the mushrooms are cooked and the spinach has wilted. Remove from the heat and set aside.

In a bowl, whisk the eggs, milk and flour together. Mix in the chopped parsley and season with salt and pepper. Transfer the vegetables from the pan to the prepared baking dish. Sprinkle the feta over the layer of vegetables, then pour in the egg mixture and top with the pumpkin seeds. Bake for about 25 minutes until the mixture is cooked.

Tip: Endurance athletes should add some artisan bread as the carbohydrate component of this dish.

	Per serve	Per 100 g
Energy	421 kcal	123 kcal
Protein	26.6 g	7.7 g
Fat	22.4 g	6.5 g
Carbohydrate	25.5 g	7.3 g
Iron	5.0 mg	1.4 mg

Esther Keown's Crispy Cauli Mexican Tacos

Serves 3

1 large cauliflower head,
  cut into bite-sized pieces

Peanut butter sauce
2 heaped tbsp
  peanut butter
3 tbsp coconut oil
2 tbsp honey
2 tbsp soy sauce

Breadcrumb coating
1 cup fine breadcrumbs
1 tsp garlic powder
1 tsp ground turmeric
1 tsp ground cumin
1 tsp smoked paprika
½ tsp chilli powder
Salt and pepper

Cooked beans
Olive oil for cooking
400 g can black
  beans, drained
400 g can chilli beans
400 g can crushed tomato
400 g can sweetcorn,
  drained
1 tbsp tomato paste
1 tbsp garlic powder
1 tsp smoked paprika
1 tsp dried thyme
½ tsp chilli powder
Salt and pepper

This is one of Esther's go-to dishes.

Preheat the oven to 210°C. Line an oven tray with baking paper.

For the sauce, place all the ingredients in a pot over a medium heat and stir to combine.

For the breadcrumb coating, place all the ingredients in a bowl, add a generous shake of salt and pepper and mix to combine.

Place the cauliflower in a large bowl and pour over the sauce, mixing it through until all the pieces are coated. Repeat with the breadcrumb mix (see tip).

Place the cauliflower on the prepared oven tray and bake for 30 minutes, making sure to flip the cauliflower pieces halfway through. Check if the cauliflower is soft and crispy at 30 minutes; if not you can bake it for a little longer or place under the grill for a short time to crisp up.

Meanwhile, for the beans, heat a dash of olive oil in a pot set over a medium heat. Add the black beans, chilli beans, tomato and corn, mix together then add the tomato paste, garlic powder, smoked paprika, thyme, chilli powder and salt and pepper to taste. Cook for 5-10 minutes until warmed through.

	Per serve	Per 100 g
Energy	1411 kcal	145 kcal
Protein	47.9 g	4.9 g
Fat	75.4 g	7.8 g
Carbohydrate	115.6 g	11.9 g
Iron	17.1 mg	1.8 mg

Guacamole
1 ripe avocado
Juice of ½ lemon
Salt and pepper

Cashew cheese
1 cup cashews (soaked
   overnight for softness
   or you can crush them
   from raw if you have
   a good blender)
Juice of ½ lemon
2 tbsp nutritional yeast
½ tsp garlic powder
¼ cup water

To serve
9 tacos, warmed

For the guacamole, cut open the avocado and place the flesh in a bowl, add the lemon juice, salt and pepper to taste, then mash with a fork.

For the cashew cheese, place all the ingredients in a food processor or blender and mix until you get a similar consistency to sour cream. If the cashew cheese is too thick, add a teaspoon of water at a time until you get your desired consistency.

Serve each taco filled with a handful of cauliflower, a gengerous spoon of bean mix, some guacamole and cashew cheese.

Tip: When you're adding the breadcrumb coating, do it slowly and when you are satisfied with the coverage on the cauliflower you can stop and save the rest in a container for the next time you make this. If you like it extra crispy add the whole breadcrumb coating.

Pulled Jackfruit Burgers

Nothing beats the flavour and texture of pulled jackfruit. Once it is made, you can keep it in the fridge for a few days and use it for other dishes, such as tacos, baked potatoes and wraps.

Serves 4 athletes

Pulled jackfruit

1 tbsp olive oil
1 small red onion,
  finely chopped
1 tsp ground cinnamon
1 tsp ground cumin
2 tsp smoked paprika
1 tsp chilli powder
¼ cup barbecue sauce
1 tbsp apple cider vinegar
200 g chopped tomatoes
2 x 400 g cans young
  jackfruit, drained well
  and excess liquid
  squeezed out

To serve

4 large buns
Spinach leaves
½ red onion, sliced
Vegan Aioli (see page
  105) or regular aioli

Heat the oil in a frying pan over a medium heat. Add the onion and cook for a few minutes to soften. Add the spices and cook for 2-3 minutes. Add the barbecue sauce and vinegar and mix well. Add the tomatoes, then stir in the jackfruit. Leave to simmer gently, covered, for 20 minutes, stirring occasionally. Take the lid off and cook for a further 10 minutes. Shred the jackfruit with two forks.

Assemble the burger buns with the pulled jackfruit and the spinach, red onion and aioli.

Tip: Power athletes could add some extra protein to assist their protein pulsing.

	Per serve	Per 100 g
Energy	553 kcal	128 kcal
Protein	15.0 g	3.5 g
Fat	11.5 g	2.7 g
Carbohydrate	92.7 g	21.4 g
Iron	4.4 mg	1.0 mg

Kūmara, Lentil and Halloumi Pie

Satisfying and tasty — sure to become a household favourite.

Serves 4 athletes

Pastry

1¾ cups gluten-free
  or plain flour
110 g butter
1 free-range egg
1 tsp salt
2 tbsp water

Pie filling

Oil for frying
1 brown onion, diced
1 tsp minced garlic
6 mushrooms, sliced
1 large orange kūmara, *sw potato*
  peeled and grated
180 g halloumi, diced
  into cubes
400 g can lentils, drained
2 tbsp sweet chilli sauce
4–5 free-range
  eggs, whisked
1 handful of spinach leaves

To serve

Green salad

Preheat the oven to 180ºC fan bake. Oil a large pie dish (approx. 24 cm diameter).

For the pastry, place all the ingredients in a food processor and whizz until the mixture forms a clump (you may need to add extra water or flour if it is too wet or dry). Transfer to the fridge for 5-10 minutes.

For the pie filling, heat some oil in a large frying pan. Add the onion and garlic and sauté for a few minutes to soften. Add the mushrooms and continue to cook until soft, then add the grated kūmara and cook for about 5 minutes more. Take off the heat and transfer the mixture to a large bowl. Add the halloumi, lentils, sweet chilli sauce, eggs and spinach and mix to combine.

Roll out the chilled pastry so that it will cover the bottom and sides of the pie dish. Fill the pastry with the pie mixture. Bake for about 30 minutes, or until the egg mixture has cooked.

Serve the pie with a green salad.

	Per serve	Per 100 g
Energy	896 kcal	166 kcal
Protein	39.8 g	7.4 g
Fat	38.5 g	7.1 g
Carbohydrate	90.5 g	16.7 g
Iron	6.2 mg	1.2 mg

Black Bean and Salsa Enchiladas

VEGAN OPTION

This is a quick and easy go-to dinner. The home-made salsa is fresh and 100 times tastier than anything store-bought!

Serves 2–3 athletes

Salsa
2–3 tomatoes, diced
¼ red onion, diced
Drizzle of olive oil
Juice of 1 lime
Salt and pepper

Enchiladas
2 x 400 g cans black
   chilli beans (or any chilli
   bean alternative)
1 cup frozen peas and corn
   mix (or fresh if you have it)
2 handfuls of spinach
1 cup grated cheese
   or vegan cheese
   of your choice
10 tortilla wraps
Coriander, to garnish

To serve
Green salad

Preheat the oven to 180ºC fan bake.

For the salsa, place all the ingredients in a bowl and mix well to combine.

For the enchiladas, heat the black beans, frozen peas and corn, spinach, half the cheese and half the salsa in a pot until warm. Assemble the enchiladas by placing a generous spoonful of filling on each tortilla wrap. Roll up each wrap and lay side by side in a baking dish that will fit them tightly. Spread the remaining salsa and cheese on top. Bake for 20 minutes or until the wraps are crispy and cheese is golden.

Garnish the enchiladas with coriander and serve with a green salad on the side.

Tip: Add some starchy vegetables to increase the carbohydrate component of this meal if you use it for recovery.

	Per serve	Per 100 g
Energy	812 kcal	133 kcal
Protein	34.0 g	5.7 g
Fat	25.0 g	4.2 g
Carbohydrate	99.1 g	16.2 g
Iron	6.6 mg	1.1 mg

Justina Kitchen's 10-minute Spaghetti 'Kind-of' Bolognaise

VEGAN

Justina is a highly competent windsurfer and kiteboarder. Her long-term target is the 2024 Paris Olympics where kite foiling will be contested for the first time. She is also the mother of two beautiful young girls. This quick and easy recipe is a staple in her busy household. And . . . pasta is the way to every athlete's heart!

Serves 3 hungry or 4 regular athletes

500 g spaghetti
Olive oil for drizzling
  and cooking
1 onion, chopped
1 tbsp mixed herbs
Salt and pepper
400 g can chickpeas,
  drained
400 g can brown lentils
2 x 400 g cans
  cherry tomatoes
400 g can whole
  peeled tomatoes
1 carrot, grated (peeled
  first if desired)
2 handfuls of spinach
  leaves, roughly chopped
Vegan Parmesan (optional)

Cook the spaghetti in a large pot of boiling water according to the packet instructions. Drain and mix a little olive oil into the spaghetti to stop it sticking together. Meanwhile, heat a dash of olive oil in a large pot over a medium heat. Add the onion and cook for a few minutes to soften. Add the mixed herbs, salt and pepper and cook for another 1-2 minutes. Add the chickpeas and brown lentils and cook for 1-2 minutes. Add the cherry tomatoes and peeled tomatoes. Crush the whole peeled tomatoes using a wooden spoon as they cook. Simmer for 5-6 minutes. Add the carrot and spinach while the tomatoes are simmering.

Serve the spaghetti with the sauce topped with a sprinkle of vegan Parmesan, if desired.

Tip: You can use any veggies in the sauce, just make sure they'll cook in a few minutes.

	Per serve	Per 100 g
Energy	948 kcal	132 kcal
Protein	40.4 g	5.6 g
Fat	9.7 g	1.4 g
Carbohydrate	162.7 g	22.7 g
Iron	11.0 mg	1.5 mg

Miso Pumpkin Pasta

VEGAN

This pumpkin pasta dish is so good! We love the mix of salty and sweet flavours. It's also an excellent recovery meal as it contains plenty of good-quality carbohydrates.

Serves 4 athletes

Pumpkin sauce

½ pumpkin, diced (to yield about 2 cups mashed)
2 tbsp olive oil
300 g any pasta or vegan pasta
2 tbsp miso paste
2 tsp minced garlic
1 tsp minced chilli
2 tbsp peanut butter
1 tbsp soy sauce
400 g can chickpeas, drained
Large handful of spinach leaves

To serve

Toasted pumpkin and sesame seeds

Preheat the oven to 180ºC. Line a baking tray with baking paper.

Place the pumpkin on the tray and drizzle with the olive oil. Roast for about 30 minutes or until golden. Remove from the oven and set aside to cool. Place the cooled pumpkin in a bowl and mash with a fork.

Meanwhile, cook the pasta in a pot of boiling water according to the packet instructions until al dente. Drain, reserving ½ cup of the cooking water.

Add the miso paste, garlic, chilli, peanut butter and soy sauce to the pumpkin and mix well. Add enough of the reserved pasta cooking water to form a smooth sauce.

Mix together the pasta, pumpkin sauce, chickpeas and spinach in a large pot or wok and cook until heated through.

Serve the pasta topped with toasted pumpkin and sesame seeds.

Tip: If you require a little more protein you could top with some pan-fried halloumi.

	Per serve	Per 100 g
Energy	638 kcal	176 kcal
Protein	24.0 g	6.6 g
Fat	29.3 g	8.1 g
Carbohydrate	62.5 g	17.2 g
Iron	5.7 mg	1.6 mg

Kūmara and Chickpea Burger with Avo Slaw

Avo slaw is a game changer! It is a mix of guacamole and coleslaw and makes this burger a 10 out of 10.

Makes 8 burgers

Patties

1 large orange kūmara, peeled and diced into 2 cm cubes
400 g can chickpeas, drained
1 free-range egg
1 cup flour of your choice
1 tsp minced garlic
½ tsp ground cumin
½ tsp dried oregano
Salt and pepper
Oil for cooking

Slaw

2 avocados, peeled and pitted
1 tomato, diced
½ red onion, finely diced
½ red capsicum, thinly sliced
2 handfuls of shredded red or green cabbage
4 gherkins, sliced
⅛ cup gherkin juice
2 tbsp lemon juice
2 tbsp sweet chilli sauce
2 tbsp mayo
Salt and pepper

To serve

8 thick slices of Edam cheese
8 burger buns

For the patties, place the kūmara in a pot of water. Bring it to the boil and cook until soft. Remove from the pot and set aside to cool. Place the cooled kūmara in a food processor with the chickpeas and egg and whizz until smooth. Add the flour, garlic, cumin, oregano, salt and pepper and whizz until combined. Flour your hands and shape the mixture into 8 patties. Heat some oil over a medium heat in a cast iron skillet. Add 4 of the patties and shallow-fry them for about 4 minutes on each side. When the patties are almost cooked on the second side, top each patty with a slice of cheese and allow to slightly melt.

For the slaw, place the avocado in a large bowl and mash. Add the tomato, red onion, capsicum, cabbage and gherkins. Add the gherkin juice, lemon juice, sweet chilli sauce and mayo and mix to combine. Season to taste with salt and pepper.

Split and fill each burger bun with a patty and some slaw.

Tip: Athletes with high energy requirements should have more than one burger to ensure they consume sufficient carbohydrate and protein.

	Per serve	Per 100 g
Energy	320 kcal	111 kcal
Protein	11.8 g	4.1 g
Fat	11.8 g	4.1 g
Carbohydrate	38.0 g	13.2 g
Iron	2.4 mg	0.8 mg

Hugo Inglis' Black Pepper Mushroom and Tofu

VEGAN

Hugo is a talented hockey player and the type of person that inspires those around him to think outside the box. This recipe is seriously yum — we love the crispy tofu!

Serves 4 athletes

600–800 g medium or firm
  tofu (preferably organic)
½ cup cornflour
Olive oil for shallow-frying
100 g vegan butter
4 brown onions,
  thinly sliced
6 tsp minced garlic
2 red chillies, chopped
3 tbsp chopped ginger
6–8 mushrooms, sliced
1 red capsicum, diced
6 tbsp soy sauce
2 tbsp caster sugar (or
  honey/maple syrup/
  agave syrup)
2 tsp crushed black
  peppercorns

To serve
4 spring onions,
  thinly sliced

Prepare the tofu by draining the liquid and wrapping it in paper towels to remove any excess liquid. While the tofu is drying, place the cornflour on a plate. Pour enough oil into a large frying pan to come about 5 mm up the sides and heat on medium-to-high. Chop the tofu into large cubes (3 cm x 2 cm). Toss the cubes in the cornflour and transfer them to the frying pan (they may need to be fried in 2 batches so they don't stew). Fry the cubes, turning, until they have a golden crust, then transfer them to paper towels.

Remove the oil and sediment from the pan, then add the vegan butter and melt. Add the onions, garlic, chillies and ginger. Sauté on a low-to-medium heat for about 10 minutes. Add the mushrooms, capsicum, soy sauce and caster sugar and stir well. Add the crushed black pepper. Cook over a medium heat for around 5 minutes (if the pan starts to dry out, add a little bit of water to the mixture). Add the tofu to warm it through, cooking for another 1-2 minutes. Cook your rice noodles according to the packet directions.

Dish up the noodles into separate bowls, top with the tofu mix and garnish with the spring onions.

	Per serve	Per 100 g
Energy	635 kcal	128 kcal
Protein	26.5 g	5.3 g
Fat	36.3 g	7.3 g
Carbohydrate	45.2 g	9.1 g
Iron	9.3 mg	1.9 mg

Root Vegetable Tagine

This winter warmer can be made in the slow cooker so you have a delish dinner to come home to! It's a flexi recipe that can be adapted to use any seasonal vegetables.

Serves 6 athletes

Curry

1 brown onion, diced into 2 cm cubes
1 tsp minced garlic
1 tsp minced chilli
2 tbsp olive oil
400 g can chickpeas, drained
2 x 400 g cans chopped tomatoes
1 cup pitted prunes
1 parsnip, peeled and diced into 2 cm cubes
1 kūmara, peeled and diced into 2 cm cubes
8 yams, diced into 2 cm cubes
1 carrot, diced into 2 cm cubes
¼ pumpkin, diced into 2 cm cubes
1 cup vegetable stock
1 tsp ground turmeric
1 tsp cajun spice mix
1 tsp dried oregano
1 tsp ground cumin

Couscous

1½ cups water
1 cup couscous
1 tsp butter

To serve

Raisins or sultanas

Slow cooker:
Place all the ingredients for the curry in a slow cooker and mix well with a spoon. Cook on low for 6-8 hours or on high for 3-4 hours, stirring occasionally.

Stovetop:
Place all ingredients in a large cast iron pot and cook on low for 1 hour or until the vegetables are soft.

For the couscous, bring the water to the boil in a small pot. Remove from the heat and add the couscous and butter. Mix with a fork and leave to absorb for 10 minutes.

Serve the tagine with couscous and a sprinkling of raisins or sultanas

Tip: This is an excellent dish to top up your depleted glycogen stores after a long training session. Power athletes should consider adding a little bit more protein (nuts and/or seeds) to this dish.

	Per serve	Per 100 g
Energy	491 kcal	87.3 kcal
Protein	15.5 g	2.8 g
Fat	8.4 g	1.5 g
Carbohydrate	83.6 g	14.7 g
Iron	4.1 g	0.7 mg

Mushroom and Leek Risotto

A leek in a risotto is much better than a leek in a boat.

Serves 4 athletes

1 cup sliced mushrooms
2 cups water
1 litre vegetable stock
  (made with 2 stock
  cubes, or you can
  make your own)
1-2 tbsp butter or oil
1 large leek or 2 small
  leeks, sliced
1 cup arborio rice
2 cloves garlic,
  finely chopped
¾ cup grated cheese (or
  ¼ cup if using Parmesan)
2 cups chopped baby
  spinach leaves
Zest of ½ lemon
Salt and pepper

To serve (optional)
⅓ cup grated Parmesan
1 handful of chopped
  parsley

In a small pot, heat the water over a medium heat. Once simmering, add the stock and reduce heat to low.

In the meantime, heat a large frying pan over a medium heat and add 1 tablespoon of butter or oil. Add the mushrooms to the pan and sauté, stirring frequently, until tender and slightly browned, 3-4 minutes. Add the remaining butter or oil to the pan with the sliced leeks. Sauté for 1-2 minutes or until softened and very slightly browned. Add the rice, and cook for 1 minute, stirring occasionally, to coat. Add the warmed stock to the pan, ½ cup at a time, stirring almost constantly, giving the risotto little breaks to come back to a simmer. You want the mixture to be cooking but not boiling or it will get gummy and cook too fast. Keep adding the stock, stirring to incorporate, until the rice is 'al dente'. You may need to add more water; adjust as appropriate.

Once the rice is cooked through, remove from heat. Add the cheese and baby spinach and stir through. Add the lemon zest and season with salt and pepper.

To serve, divide between serving bowls and top with a sprinkle of Parmesan and parsley, if desired. Alternatively, for extra protein, add ½ cup feta and ½ cup toasted walnuts.

	Per serve	Per 100 g
Energy	422 kcal	96 kcal
Protein	18.6 g	4.2 g
Fat	18.6 g	4.1 g
Carbohydrate	43.6 g	10.0 g
Iron	1.0 mg	0.2 mg

Spicy Chickpea Curry

This is the best easy curry recipe — perfect when you've been training hard all day. An ideal meal for an athlete as it has great quantities of both protein and carbohydrates.

Serves 4 athletes

Rice
½ cup uncooked
  rice per person
1 cup water per every
  ½ cup uncooked rice
1 tsp salt

Curry
Oil for cooking
1 brown onion, diced
2 tsp minced garlic
6 minced, sliced
2 x 400 g cans
  crushed tomatoes
400 g can chickpeas,
  drained
2–3 tomatoes, chopped,
  or a handful of
  cherry tomatoes
180–200 g halloumi, diced
2 tsp ground cumin
1 tsp chilli flakes (optional)
1 head of broccoli, cut
  into small florets or 2
  handfuls of spinach

For the rice, put the rice, water and salt into a pot. Bring to the boil and immediately take off the heat. Leave for 10 minutes to absorb the water. Fluff up with a fork before serving.

For the curry, heat some oil in a large frying pan. Add the onion, garlic and mushrooms and sauté over a medium heat for a few minutes to brown. Add the canned tomatoes, chickpeas, fresh tomatoes, halloumi, cumin and chilli flakes, if using. Cook over a low heat for around 15 minutes. Add the broccoli or spinach 5 minutes before serving and continue to cook over a low heat.

Serve the curry with the rice.

Tip: Endurance athletes should add some extra rice.

	Per serve	Per 100 g
Energy	712 kcal	82 kcal
Protein	30.8 g	3.5 g
Fat	14.9 g	1.7 g
Carbohydrate	109.0 g	12.6 g
Iron	5.6 mg	0.6 mg

Lentil and Cheese Pie

Pies are a favourite in our houses, especially this one, which is full of veggies.

Serves 6 athletes

Pastry
1¾ cups flour
110 g butter
1 free-range egg
1 tsp salt
2 tbsp water

Filling
Oil for cooking
1 brown onion, diced
2 tsp minced garlic
1 tsp minced chilli
8–10 mushrooms, sliced
2 tomatoes, diced
1–2 carrots, grated
  (peeled first if desired)
½ cup frozen peas
¼ cup tomato paste
400 g can lentils

Cheese sauce
50 g butter
2 tbsp flour
¾ cup milk
Large handful of grated
  Edam or Colby cheese

To serve
Green salad

Preheat the oven to 180°C. Oil a 24-cm diameter pie dish.

For the pastry, place all the ingredients in a food processor and blitz until the mixture forms a clump (you may need to add extra water or flour, depending on if it is wet or dry). Transfer the pastry to the fridge to chill for 5–10 minutes.

For the filling, heat some oil in a large frying pan. Add the onion, garlic and chilli and sauté for a few minutes until the onion is soft. Add the mushrooms and continue to cook until soft. Add the tomatoes, carrots, peas, tomato paste and lentils. Cook until everything is soft and combined. Remove from the heat and set aside to cool.

For the cheese sauce, melt the butter in a pot over a medium heat. Stir in the flour and cook, stirring continuously, for 1–2 minutes. Gradually whisk in the milk, adding a little at a time, and continue to cook to form a thick sauce. Take off the heat and add the grated cheese, stirring until it is melted.

To assemble the pie, roll three-quarters of the chilled pastry out and fit to the bottom and sides of the pie dish. Add the filling mixture and evenly spread the cheese sauce over the top. Roll out the remaining pastry and place on top, curling the edges to seal. Bake for about 30 minutes or until golden. Serve with a green salad.

Tip: If you are an endurance athlete, you might like to add some starchy vegetables (pumpkin, potato, kūmara) to the pie filling.

	Per serve	Per 100 g
Energy	546 kcal	152 kcal
Protein	21.2 g	5.9 g
Fat	29.3 g	8.1 g
Carbohydrate	43.1 g	12.0 g
Iron	3.4 mg	0.9 mg

Saag Paneer

This one is super-tasty and full
of so much goodness.

Serves 4 athletes

Rice

½ cup uncooked
  rice per person
1 cup water per every
  ½ cup uncooked rice
1 tsp salt

Curry

¼ cup oil
1 brown onion, diced
1 tbsp minced garlic
2 tsp minced ginger
1 tsp minced chilli or 1 tsp
  chilli flakes (optional)
2 tsp ground cumin
2 tsp garam masala
¼ tsp cayenne pepper
1 tsp salt
Pepper
½ cup water
500 g frozen spinach
1½ cups cream or
  coconut cream
300 g paneer, diced

For the rice, put the rice, water and salt into a pot. Bring to the boil and immediately take off the heat. Leave for 10 minutes to absorb the water. Fluff up with a fork before serving.

For the curry, heat 2 tablespoons of the oil in a large frying pan. Add the onion and sauté for a few minutes to soften. Add the garlic, ginger and chilli, if using, and continue to sauté. Add the remaining oil and mix in the cumin, garam masala, cayenne pepper, salt and pepper until it forms a paste. Add the water and frozen spinach and cook over a low heat until the spinach has thawed. Add cream and simmer for 10–15 minutes.

While the curry is simmering, pan-fry the paneer until it is crispy on both sides.

Serve the paneer on top of curry and rice.

	Per serve	Per 100 g
Energy	1027 kcal	137 kcal
Protein	23.6 g	3.2 g
Fat	62.5 g	8.4 g
Carbohydrate	88.2 g	11.8 g
Iron	5.2 mg	0.7 mg

Ricotta and Spinach Gnocchi

The easiest gnocchi you'll ever make (no peeling a sack of potatoes!). We have even found that our toddler friends love it too.

Serves 3 athletes

Gnocchi

2 handfuls of
 spinach leaves
400 g (1½ cups) ricotta
3 free-range egg yolks
1 cup flour of your choice
1 tsp salt
Pepper
1 cup grated cheese
 (Parmesan or Edam
 works well)
Oil for cooking

Tomato zucchini sauce

1 brown onion, sliced
2 tsp minced garlic
2 zucchini, sliced
6 mushrooms, sliced
400 g can crushed
 tomatoes
2 tbsp tomato paste
1 tsp dried oregano
1 tsp chilli paste (optional)

For the gnocchi, wilt the spinach in a large cast-iron frying pan. Remove from heat and place in a mixing bowl. Add the ricotta, egg yolks, flour, salt and pepper and mix well to combine. Mix through ¾ cup of the cheese. Form the mixture into small balls (you might need to flour your hands), put on a plate and leave in the fridge for 10 minutes to firm up. Heat some oil in the frying pan and pan-fry the gnocchi in batches, turning regularly to brown all sides. As the gnocchi is cooked, remove from the pan and set aside on a plate.

For the sauce, heat some oil in a frying pan. Add the onion and garlic and sauté until soft. Add the zucchini and mushrooms and continue cooking for a few minutes more until the zucchini is soft. Add the tomatoes, tomato paste, oregano and chilli paste, if using, and continue cooking for 5-10 minutes until the sauce has reduced a little.

Preheat the oven to 180°C. Remove the tomato sauce from the heat, add the gnocchi, sprinkle over the remaining ¼ cup cheese and crack some extra pepper on top. Bake in the oven for 5-10 minutes or until the cheese is golden.

	Per serve	Per 100 g
Energy	616 kcal	92 kcal
Protein	36.2 g	5.4 g
Fat	28.1 g	4.2 g
Carbohydrate	46.9 g	7.0 g
Iron	5.4 mg	0.8 mg

Kūmara, Lentil and Coconut Dahl

VEGAN

You'll have this recipe memorised in no time! It's a good one to make for meat-eating friends who won't even realise it's vegan.

Serves 4 athletes

Rice
½ cup uncooked
  rice per person
1 cup water per every
  ½ cup uncooked rice
1 tsp salt
½ x 400 ml can
  coconut milk

Dahl
Oil for cooking
1 brown onion, diced
2 tsp minced garlic
1 tsp ground cumin
1 tsp curry powder
1 tsp paprika
1 tsp ground turmeric
2–3 tomatoes, diced
1 large kūmara, peeled
  and cubed
400 g can lentils, drained
1½ x 400 ml cans
  coconut milk
1 tsp chilli flakes (optional)
Coriander, to garnish

For the rice, put the rice, water and salt into a pot. Bring to the boil, then immediately take off the heat and add the coconut milk. Leave for 10 minutes to absorb the liquid. Fluff up with a fork before serving.

For the dahl, heat some oil in a large frying pan, add the onion and garlic and fry until the onion is golden. Add the spices and, if necessary, a little more oil to make a paste and fry for 1 minute. Add the tomatoes and fry for another minute. Add the kūmara, lentils, coconut milk and chilli flakes, if using. Stir to combine, then simmer on a low heat, uncovered, for 30 minutes, keeping an eye on it and stirring regularly.

Serve the dahl with the rice and garnish with coriander.

Tip: Serve this with steamed broccoli and 1 tbsp sour cream per person for an extra protein hit.

	Per serve	Per 100 g
Energy	488 kcal	80 kcal
Protein	17.3 g	2.8 g
Fat	18.6 g	3.0 g
Carbohydrate	61.2 g	9.1 g
Iron	6.8 mg	1.1 mg

Mushroom Fettuccine

A yum staple to have on the menu.

Serves 4 athletes

3 tbsp butter
1 brown onion, diced
1 tsp dried rosemary
1 tbsp minced garlic
6 large mushrooms, sliced
3 cups vegetable stock
1 cup cream
340 g fettuccine pasta
   (or rice and quinoa
   gluten-free spaghetti)
1 head of broccoli,
   chopped into
   small pieces
½ cup grated Parmesan
1 large handful of
   spinach leaves
Salt and pepper

To serve (optional)
1 tsp truffle oil
2 tbsp nutritional
   yeast (see note)

Melt the butter in a large frying pan. Add the onion, rosemary and garlic and sauté for a few minutes. Add the mushrooms and cook for a few more minutes until they are soft. Add the vegetable stock, cream and pasta. Cook over a low heat until the pasta has nearly cooked and the sauce has reduced and thickened (approx. 20 minutes). Add the broccoli and continue to cook for a few more minutes. Mix through the cheese until melted, add the spinach and season with salt and pepper.

Serve the fettuccine sprinkled with truffle oil and nutritional yeast, if desired.

Note: Nutritional yeast is packed with B-vitamins, which are among the nutrients that a plant-based diet can often be low in.

	Per serve	Per 100 g
Energy	751 kcal	145 kcal
Protein	23.3 g	4.5 g
Fat	43.2 g	8.3 g
Carbohydrate	61.4 g	12.4 g
Iron	3.3 mg	0.6 mg

Ashlee Rowe's Butter Chickpeas and Coconut Rice

VEGAN

Honestly, this is so good; Ash is a legend for coming up with it. It is so close to tasting like a store-bought curry without all the preservatives and additives.

Serves 4 athletes

Coconut rice
½ cup uncooked
  rice per person
1 cup water per every
  ½ cup uncooked rice
1 tsp salt
½ x 400 ml can
  coconut cream

Curry
2 tbsp olive oil
1 brown onion, diced
4 tsp paprika
2 tsp ground cumin
1 tsp turmeric
1 tsp minced garlic
6–7 mushrooms, sliced
400 g can chickpeas,
  drained
410 g can tomato purée
½ x 400 ml can
  coconut cream
¼ cup brown sugar
½ tsp salt
Pepper
½ tsp chilli flakes (optional)
2–3 handfuls of
  spinach leaves

For the coconut rice, put the rice, water and salt into a pot. Bring to the boil, then immediately take off the heat and add the coconut cream. Leave for 10 minutes to absorb the liquid. Fluff up with a fork before serving.

Heat most of the olive oil in a large frying pan. Add the onion and sauté for a few minutes. Add a little more oil with the paprika, cumin, turmeric and garlic and fry until fragrant. Add the mushrooms and chickpeas and stir to coat with the spices. Mix in the tomato purée, coconut cream, brown sugar, salt, pepper, and chilli flakes, if using. Simmer over a low heat for about 20 minutes. Mix through the spinach.

Serve the curry with the coconut rice.

Tip: This meal will provide you with great fuel for your tough training sessions as it contains sufficient good-quality carbohydrates.

	Per serve	Per 100 g
Energy	767 kcal	101 kcal
Protein	21.2 g	2.8 g
Fat	24.4 g	3.2 g
Carbohydrate	112.7 g	14.7 g
Iron	5.8 mg	0.8 mg

Luuka's Raw Snack Bars

VEGAN

The perfect energy hit that keeps me performing at my best.

Makes 10 bars

½ cup buckwheat
1 cup desiccated coconut
½ cup protein powder
¼ cup chia seeds
½ cup pumpkin seeds
   (or a mix of pumpkin
   and sunflower seeds)
6 tbsp coconut oil
¼ cup cocoa powder
⅓ cup liquid sweetener
   (maple syrup/
   coconut syrup)
⅓ cup oats

Line a 20 cm x 20 cm dish with baking paper.

Place the buckwheat in a pan set over a medium heat and toast until lightly golden.

Transfer the buckwheat to a food processor and add the remaining ingredients, except for the oats. Pulse until mixed together but don't overmix — you still want a bit of crunch. Add the oats and mix through with a spoon.

Transfer the mixture to the prepared dish and compress it with the back of a spoon. Put in the fridge for 30 minutes before cutting into bars. Store in a container in the fridge for up to a week.

	Per serve	Per 100 g
Energy	287 kcal	494 kcal
Protein	7.1 g	12.2 g
Fat	21.5 g	27.0 g
Carbohydrate	16.0 g	27.5 g
Iron	2.2 mg	3.8 mg

Peanut Butter and Chocolate Oat Cookies

These cookies are a yum pre- or post-training snack and we often find we have most of these ingredients at home so they can be made whenever.

Makes 20 cookies (depending on how much dough you eat)

½ cup crunchy
  peanut butter
1 egg
½ cup honey
1 cup quick oats
1 cup flour of your choice
1½ tsp baking powder
¼ tsp baking soda
½ tsp salt
¾ cup chocolate buttons

Preheat the oven to 180°C. Bake and line an oven tray with baking paper.

Place the peanut butter, egg and honey in a large bowl and mix until combined. Add the oats, flour, baking powder, baking soda, salt and chocolate buttons to the wet ingredients and mix to combine. Once a dough has formed, cover the bowl and leave in the fridge for at least 30 minutes (and up to a day). Remove the mixture from the fridge. Wet your hands and mould the cookie dough into 20 balls. Place on the prepared oven tray and lightly flatten with a floured fork. Bake for 10-12 minutes or until golden, then set aside to cool.

Serve with your favourite milk!

Tips: Two biscuits and a big glass of milk could double as a recovery snack for most athletes.

The cookie dough can be made and formed into balls and stored in the freezer until you are ready to bake them.

	Per cookie	Per 100 g
Energy	165 kcal	420 kcal
Protein	4.1 g	10.3 g
Fat	7.2 g	18.3 g
Carbohydrate	20.7 g	53.1 g
Iron	0.5 mg	1.4 mg

Kerri Gowler's Muesli Slice

VEGAN OPTION

Oats move boats, right Kerri? This double Olympic medallist brought home both a gold and silver medal from the Tokyo Olympics. Her talents are endless, and we are stoked that she has shared her muesli slice with us!

Makes 10 squares

½ cup peanut butter
2 heaped tbsp coconut oil
¼ cup maple syrup
  or honey
2 cups oats
½ cup sunflower seeds
½ cup pumpkin seeds
¼ cup flaxseeds
¼ cup shredded coconut
¾ cup chopped dates

Line a baking dish with baking paper.

Place the peanut butter, coconut oil and maple syrup in a large pot set over a medium heat and melt together. Remove from the heat and mix through all the other ingredients. Transfer to the prepared baking dish and pat flat. Chill in the fridge for 1-2 hours to set. Once set, slice into 10 squares and store in an airtight container for up to 1 week.

	Per serve	Per 100 g
Energy	409 kcal	449 kcal
Protein	13.0 g	14.2 g
Fat	22.1 g	24.1 g
Carbohydrate	41.0 g	44.9 g
Iron	3.0 mg	3.2 mg

Black Bean Cookies

VEGAN

Who would have thought black beans work in cookies? Trust us, these are good!

Makes approx. 10 cookies

350 g cooked black
   beans (or 400 g
   can black beans,
   drained and rinsed)
2 tbsp cocoa powder
⅓ cup liquid sweetener
   (maple syrup/coconut
   syrup/honey)
2 tbsp coconut oil
¼ cup shredded coconut
1 tbsp chia seeds
1 cup porridge oats
½ tsp baking powder
½ cup chopped
   dark chocolate

Preheat the oven to 180°C. Line a baking tray with baking paper.

Place the beans in a food processor with the cocoa powder and sweetener and pulse until smooth. Add the rest of the ingredients, except for the dark chocolate, and pulse until mixed. Add the dark chocolate and mix through with a spoon. Scoop out spoonfuls of the mixture and roll into balls. Place the balls on the prepared baking tray and flatten into cookie shapes. Bake for 15-20 minutes.

	Per serve	Per 100 g
Energy	226 kcal	299 kcal
Protein	5.5 g	7.2 g
Fat	12.3 g	16.2 g
Carbohydrate	21.9 g	28.8 g
Iron	2.2 mg	2.9 mg

Raw Carrot Cake

VEGAN

For those of us who aren't very good at baking cakes.

Serves 10

Carrot cake
1 cup pitted dates
1 cup walnuts
½ cup desiccated coconut
2–4 tsp cinnamon
Pinch of salt
4 carrots, grated (peeled first if desired)

Cashew icing
1 cup cashews
¼ cup water
3 tbsp maple syrup
1 tsp vanilla essence
Juice of ½ lemon
⅓ cup melted coconut oil
Pinch of salt

Before starting, soak the dates in a bowl of boiling water with a plate over the top for approximately 15 minutes. Do the same in another bowl with the cashew nuts. Line a 23 cm x 12 cm loaf tin with baking paper.

For the carrot cake, drain the dates and place in a food processor with the walnuts, coconut, cinnamon and salt. Blend to combine. Add the carrot and blend until fully combined. Scrape the mixture into the prepared loaf tin and press to smooth. Place in the fridge to chill while making the icing.

For the cashew icing, drain the cashews and place in a food processor with the water, maple syrup, vanilla essence, lemon juice, coconut oil and a pinch of salt.

Remove the cake from the fridge and spoon the icing on top. Cover and place back in the fridge for at least 2 hours to set.

Tip: If you add a dollop of yoghurt to this yummy carrot cake, you will be provided with some protein and carbs throughout your day.

	Per serve	Per 100 g
Energy	346 kcal	276 kcal
Protein	5.0 g	4.0 g
Fat	26.2 g	17.6 g
Carbohydrate	22.1 g	17.6 g
Iron	1.6 mg	1.3 mg

Chickpea Mousse

VEGAN

Just three ingredients . . . and so bloody good. We like making our friends guess the key ingredient.

Serves 6 athletes

½ cup aquafaba (the brine drained
  from canned chickpeas)
120 g 50% cocoa dark chocolate
1 tbsp maple syrup

Whisk the aquafaba with an electric mixer until light and fluffy. Melt the chocolate in a double boiler on the stove, or melt it in the microwave, making sure to heat it in short bursts while mixing regularly. In a bowl, fold the whisked aquafaba, melted chocolate and maple syrup together. Divide between 6 small ramekins and leave to chill in the fridge for 3 hours or overnight.

	Per serve	Per 100 g
Energy	199 kcal	216 kcal
Protein	5 g	5.4 g
Fat	12.3 g	13.3 g
Carbohydrate	16.9 g	18.3 g
Iron	2.3 mg	2.4 mg

Silken Tofu Mousse

VEGAN

This is a yummy protein-packed dessert!

Serves 6 athletes

150 g 50% cocoa dark chocolate
350 g silken tofu (see tip)
2 tbsp maple syrup
¼ cup of your favourite tea, brewed (Earl
  grey, green tea, English breakfast, etc.)

Melt the chocolate in a double boiler on the stove, or melt it in the microwave, making sure to heat it in short bursts while mixing regularly. Place the melted chocolate, tofu, maple syrup and tea in a food processor and blitz until combined and smooth. Divide between 6 small ramekins and leave to chill in the fridge for 3 hours or overnight.

Tip: You'll find silken tofu in the pantry aisle, not the fridge.

	Per serve	Per 100 g
Energy	160 kcal	554 kcal
Protein	1.8	6.3 g
Fat	10.8	36.7 g
Carbohydrate	13.6	46.2 g
Iron	1.15 mg	3.9 mg

Bliss Balls

VEGAN

Makes about 15 balls

We like bliss balls as an alternative to store-bought muesli bars to cut down plastic waste. These also freeze well.

Apricot and Cashew

1 cup dried apricots
¼ cup chia seeds + ½ cup boiling water
1 cup cashews
½ cup desiccated coconut, plus extra to coat

Before starting, soak the dried apricots in a bowl of boiling water with a plate on top for about 20 minutes, then drain. Do the same in a separate bowl with the chia seeds and the boiling water, but do not drain.

Place the drained apricots and chia seeds (including water) in a food processor with the cashews and coconut and blitz to combine. You may need to add more water to get a good consistency. Scoop about a heaped tablespoon of mixture into your wet hands (wetting them makes the mixture easy to work with) and mould into a ball. Continue doing this with all the mixture. Coat the balls in desiccated coconut, if desired. Store in an airtight container in the fridge and eat within 3-4 days.

	Per ball	Per 100 g
Energy	103 kcal	404 kcal
Protein	2.4 g	9.3 g
Fat	6.5 g	25.4 g
Carbohydrate	7.5 g	29.2 g
Iron	1.0 mg	3.9 mg

Peanut Butter Date

1 cup pitted dates + ½ cup boiling water
1¼ cups almonds
1 cup rolled oats
¼ cup peanut butter
1 tbsp cocoa powder
2 tbsp water

Before starting, soak the dates in a bowl with the boiling water and a plate on top for about 20 minutes.

Place the soaked dates (including the water) in a blender with the almonds, rolled oats, peanut butter, cocoa powder, and water and blend until combined. You may need to add more water if your mixture is too dry. Scoop about a heaped tablespoon of mixture into your wet hands (wetting them makes the mixture easy to work with) and mould into a ball. Continue doing this with all the mixture. Store in an airtight container in the fridge and eat within 3-4 days.

	Per ball	Per 100 g
Energy	148 kcal	441 kcal
Protein	4.5 g	13.4 g
Fat	9.1 g	27.2 g
Carbohydrate	11.3 g	33.7 g
Iron	1.1 mg	3.3 mg

Chocolate Cashew

1 cup pitted dates + ½ cup boiling water
½ cup cashews
⅓ cup rolled oats
¼ cup honey or golden syrup
½ cup cocoa powder

Before starting, soak the dates in a bowl with the boiling water and a plate on top for about 20 minutes.

Place the soaked dates (reserve some of the water) in a blender with the cashews, rolled oats, honey and cocoa powder and blend until combined. You may need to add some of the date water if your mixture is too dry. Scoop about a heaped tablespoon of mixture into your wet hands (wetting them makes the mixture easy to work with) and mould into a ball. Continue doing this with all the mixture. Store in an airtight container in the fridge and eat within 3-4 days.

	Per ball	Per 100 g
Energy	96 kcal	377 kcal
Protein	1.7 g	6.8 g
Fat	2.7 g	10.6 g
Carbohydrate	15.4 g	60.5 g
Iron	1.5 mg	5.7 mg

Fruit Crumble

VEGAN

Crumble is our go-to dessert especially when feijoas, peaches or apples are in season. This is such a delicious, warming dessert.

Serves 8 athletes

3–4 cups fruit of your choice (apples, peaches, berries, feijoas, etc.)
½ cup coconut oil
½ cup shredded coconut
¼ cup chia seeds
½ cup brown sugar
1½ cups flour of your choice
3 tbsp maple syrup

Preheat the oven to 180°C fan bake.

Prepare the fruit and layer in an ovenproof dish. Melt the coconut oil in a small pot over a medium heat. Pour the oil into a bowl with the coconut, chia seeds, brown sugar, flour and maple syrup and mix to form a crumbly mixture. Crumble the mixture onto the fruit. Bake for 20 minutes or until the top is crispy and the fruit is hot.

Tip: To increase the protein content, we recommend serving this yummy dessert with your favourite yoghurt or ice cream.

	Per serve	Per 100 g
Energy	365 kcal	224 kcal
Protein	2.3 g	1.4 g
Fat	19.7 g	12.1 g
Carbohydrate	45.2 g	27.7 g
Iron	0.3 mg	0.2 mg

Crème Brûlée

VEGAN OPTION

This is a super quick and easy dessert.

Makes 2 brûlées

1 cup milk of your choice
3 tbsp white sugar
2 tbsp cornflour
2 tsp vanilla essence

To caramelise
2 tsp white sugar

Place the milk, sugar, cornflour and vanilla essence in a cold pot. Slowly heat over a low-to-medium heat, whisking continuously for about 5 minutes, making sure the mixture does not boil. Once the mixture has thickened, remove from the heat and divide between 2 ramekins.

Place the ramekins in the fridge for at least 2 hours to set or place in the freezer for a quicker setting time. Once set, take out of the fridge and add 1 tsp of sugar to each ramekin and caramelise with a blow torch.

	Per serve	Per 100 g
Energy	159 kcal	95 kcal
Protein	0.7 g	0.4 g
Fat	1.4 g	0.8 g
Carbohydrate	37.4 g	22.3 g
Iron	0.0 mg	0.0 mg

Luuka's Quick and Easy Bran Muffins

I make these muffins all the time. They are simple to make and a great tasty snack for when you are on the go.

Makes 6–8 medium muffins

1 cup bran
¾ cup milk
2 tbsp golden syrup
1 free-range egg, whisked
¾ cup flour, sifted
1 tsp baking soda
1½ tsp ground cinnamon

For Banana and Walnut Bran Muffins, add:

1 large (or 2 small) ripe
   banana, mashed
½ cup chopped walnuts

For Apple and Sultana Bran Muffins, add:

⅓ cup sultanas
1 medium apple, grated
   (peeled first if desired)

Preheat the oven to 200°C bake. Grease the cups of a small muffin tray.

Place the bran, milk and golden syrup in a bowl, mix together and leave to soak for 5 minutes. Add the rest of the ingredients followed by either the banana and walnuts or apple and sultanas. Spoon the mixture into the prepared muffin tray.

Bake for 15 minutes or until cooked through.

	Per serve	Per 100 g
Energy	228 kcal	241 kcal
Protein	6.7 g	7.0 g
Fat	10.5 g	9.5 g
Carbohydrate	27.8 g	29.4 g
Iron	2.3 mg	2.4 mg

Index

aerobic threshold 43
Alexandra Maloney 29
alpha-linolenic acid (ALA) 31
amino acids 24, 31
animal-based foods 10–11, 64–65
animal welfare 66
antioxidants 57
appetite regulation 48
athlete
    endurance 18, 43
    skill-based 30
    strength and power 24, 43
Beverage Hydration Index (BHI) 45, *46*
blood pressure 11
bone density 18
brain
    function 31
    nutrients 30
Brooke Francis, née Donoghue 16–17,
Brooke Neal 74, *34*
caffeine 45–47
calories 18, 20, 47
carbohydrates 12, 24, 26, 48
carbon footprint 62, 73
cardiovascular health 18, 43
carnosine 30
chicken 66
cholesterol 11
Christel Dunshea-Mooij 14–15
climate change 61
cognitive function 30, 48
cold-water immersion (CWI) 44
composting 70
compression garments 44
contrast water therapy (CWT) 44
cows 69
creatine 30
dairy products 69
Dan Smart 43
dehydration 45
diabetes 48
dietary patterns 10–11
digestion 48
docosahexaenoic acid (DHA) 31
eggs 66
electrolytes 45
eicosapentaenoic acid (EPA) 31
energy
    availability 18-19
    expenditure 20
    intake 20
    requirements 12
emissions 17
energy drink *see* sports drink
environment 10, 61
Esther Keown 76, *79*
ethical animal production 64–65, 66
Eve Macfarlane 40, 61

fat 12, 26
    mass 24
    unsaturated 12
fatigue 18, 44
fibre 12, 18, 48
flexitarian 16
'food first' policy 52
food intake 18–20, 27
Games Galore 14
gardening, vegetables 70
global warming 62
greenhouse gas emissions 62
gut
    health 48, 51
    microbiota 48
    probiotic 48
haem iron 30
heart disease 11
High Performance Sport NZ 14
homeostasis 43, 44
hormones 18
How We Got Happy 40
Hugo Inglis 74, *79*
hydration 35, 45
    Beverage Hydration Index (BHI) 45, *46*
    oral rehydration solutions 45
hydrotherapy 44
injury 18
illness 18
immune function 44, 48
inflammation 44, 51, 57
iodine 54
iron 30, 54
James Coote 61
Jim Webster 64–69
Jonathan Nabb 40
Katie Cambie 74, *79*
Kylie Wilson 42
land degradation 62
landfill 70
leucine 24, 26
LDL (low-density lipoprotein) 11
lifestyle diseases 14
Luuka Jones 22
macro nutrients 11
magnesium 12, 54
Marcus Daniell 32, 35
meal plan 20, 27, 35, 52
memory 30
menstrual function 18
menstrual cramps 57
mental fatigue 30
mental health 31, 40, 42, 48
metabolic stimulus 43, 44
metabolism 18, 19
microbiome-gut-brain axis 48
microbiota 48
micronutrients 11, 12

mindfulness 42
muscle
    fibre 43
    loss 18
    mass 18, 24, 26
    protein synthesis 24–26
    recovery, repair and growth 24, 26, 27, 44
neuromuscular activation 43, 44
nutrient-overdose-related toxicity 31
nutrition 15, 16, 22, 24, 31, 35, 52
obesity 48
ocean health 63
Omega-3 fatty acids 55
Olympic Games
    London Olympic Games 15
    Rio Olympic Games 15
    Tokyo Olympic Games 15, 45, 61
omega-3 30, 31, 55
overfishing 63
pantry staples 73
Paris Agreement 61
performance 18, 22, 45
physiological processes 18
    reproduction 18
Piera Hudson 77, *25*
plant-based foods 10–11, 24, 30, 35, 48, 52, 57, 62,
    64, 74
plastic waste 47, 63, 70, 73
power output 18
prebiotics 51, 55
probiotics 48, 55
processed foods 51
protein 11, 12, 24, 26
    intake 11, 24–27
    vegetarian sources 29, 54
psychological health 42
relative energy deficiency (RED-S) 18–19
repetition maximum (RM) 43
Ron Maughan 45
rowing 16, 61
    Rowing NZ 14
    World Championship 15
Ruby Tui 75, *79*
sailing 29
short chain fatty acids (SCFA) 51
skin health 48
sleep 44, 51
sports disciplines 12
    endurance 12
    mixed 12
    power 12
    skill 12
sports drink 31, 45–47
stress 51
stress fractures 18
supplements 30, 52
Sustainable Development Goals 61
sustainability 10, 15, 17, 47, 61–63

taurine 30, 31
tendon stiffness 43
tennis 32
third-party testing certification 52
toxins 47
training 18–19, 22, 43–44
    loads 43, 44
    periodisation 43, 44
travel 35
urine 45, *46*
vegetable gardening 70
vegetarian diet 16, 22, 29, 32, 48, 57, 62, 74
vitamin B6 30
vitamin B12 30, 52
vitamin C 12
vitamin E 12
water consumption 62
water runoff 63
well-being 42
World Anti-Doping Agency (WADA) 52
worm farm 70
zinc 54

Recipe Index

Aioli, Eggless 105
Apricot and Cashew Bliss Balls 180
Ashlee Rowe's Butter Chickpeas and Coconut Rice 167
Asian Noodle Salad 125
avocado
    Guacamole 135
    Slaw 147

Baked Beans with Yoghurt and Oat Flatbread 94
Basil and Walnut Pesto 105
beans
    Baked Beans with Yoghurt and Oat Flatbread 94
    Black Bean and Salsa Enchiladas 140
    Black Bean Cookies 174
    Beetroot Butter Bean Hummus 107
    Cooked beans 134
    Mexican beans 120
    Refried beans 127
    Shakshuka with Beans 101
beetroot
    Beetroot Butter Bean Hummus 107
    Beetroot, Feta and Brown Rice Salad 119
Berry sauce 83
biscuit, *also* bar, slice
    Black Bean Cookies 174
    Kerri Gowler's Muesli Slice 172
    Luuka's Raw Snack Bars 169
    Peanut Butter and Chocolate Oat Cookies 170
Black Bean and Salsa Enchiladas 140
Black Bean Cookies 174
bliss ball
    Apricot and Cashew 180
    Chocolate Cashew 181
    Peanut Butter Date 180
bolognaise
    Justina Kitchen's 10-minute Spaghetti 'Kind-of' Bolognaise 143
bran
    Luuka's Quick and Easy Bran Muffins 186
Breadcrumb coating 134
broccoli
    Broccoli and Mushroom Filo Log 129
    James Coote's Broccoli and Blue Cheese Soup 114
Brooke's Nana Pat's Muesli 87
Brooke's Pancakes 83
burgers
    Kūmara and Chickpea Burger with Avo Slaw 147
    Pulled Jackfruit Burgers 137

Cake, Raw Carrot 177
cashew
    Apricot and Cashew Bliss Balls 180
    Cashew cheese 135
    Cashew icing 177
    Chocolate Cashew Bliss Balls 181
cauliflower
    Esther Keown's Crispy Cauli Mexican Tacos 134
cheese

Beetroot, Feta and Brown Rice Salad 119
    Cashew cheese 135
    Cheese sauce 157
    Cheesy sauce 127
    James Coote's Broccoli and Blue Cheese Soup 114
    Lentil and Cheese Pie 157
    Pumpkin and Feta Filo Log 122
Chia Pudding 84
chickpea
    Ashlee Rowe's Butter Chickpeas and Coconut Rice 167
    Chickpea Mousse 178
    Easy Chickpea Hummus 107
    Home-made Wraps with Falafel and Greek Yoghurt Dressing 130
    Kūmara and Chickpea Burger with Avo Slaw 147
    Spicy Chickpea Curry 154
chocolate
    Chocolate Cashew Bliss Balls 181
    Peanut Butter and Chocolate Oat Cookies 170
coconut
    Coconut rice 167
    Kūmara, Lentil and Coconut Dahl 163
Cooked beans 134
Corn Fritters 97
Crème Brûlée 184
Crumble, Fruit 183
Curry, Spiced Chickpea 154

Dahl, Kūmara, Lentil and Coconut 163
dates
    Peanut Butter Date Bliss Balls 180
dressing
    Greek yoghurt dressing 130

Eggless Aioli 105
eggs
    Egg Breakfast Wraps 92
    Pickled Eggs on Toast 98
    Zucchini Slice 117
enchiladas
    Black Bean and Salsa Enchiladas 140
Energiser Smoothie 88
Esther Keown's Crispy Cauli Mexican Tacos 134

falafel
    Home-made Wraps with Falafel and Greek Yoghurt Dressing 130
filo
    Broccoli and Mushroom Filo Log 129
    Pumpkin and Feta Filo Log 122
French Toast, Savoury 91
frittata
    Potato and Spinach Frittata 132
fritters
    Corn Fritters 97
Fruit Crumble 183

Guacamole 135
Greek yoghurt dressing 130
Green Smoothie 89

halloumi
    Kūmara, Lentil and Halloumi Pie 138
Home-made Wraps with Falafel and Greek Yoghurt Dressing 130
hummus
    Beetroot Butter Bean Hummus 107
    Easy Chickpea Hummus 107
Hugo Inglis' Black Pepper Mushroom and Tofu 149

Jacket Potatoes 120
jackfruit

Pulled Jackfruit Burgers 137
James Coote's Broccoli and Blue Cheese Soup 114
Justina Kitchen's 10-minute Spaghetti 'Kind-of' Bolognaise 143

Kate Cambie's Peanut Butter Smoothie 88
Kerri Gowler's Muesli Slice 172
kūmara
    Kūmara and Chickpea Burger with Avo Slaw 147
    Kūmara, Lentil and Coconut Dahl 163
    Kūmara, Lentil and Halloumi Pie 138

Leek and Mushroom Risotto 153
lentil
    Kūmara, Lentil and Coconut Dahl 163
    Kūmara, Lentil and Halloumi Pie 138
    Lentil and Cheese Pie 157
Luuka's Raw Snack Bars 169
Luuka's Quick and Easy Bran Muffins 186

Mexican beans 120
Mexican seasoning 120
Miso Pumpkin Pasta 144
mousse
    Chickpea Mousse 178
    Silken Tofu Mousse 178
Muesli
    Brooke's Nana Pat's Muesli 87
    Kerri Gowler's Muesli Slice 172
muffins
    Luuka's Quick and Easy Bran Muffins 186
mushroom
    Broccoli and Mushroom Filo Log 129
    Hugo Inglis' Black Pepper Mushroom and Tofu 149
    Mushroom and Leek Risotto 153
    Mushroom Fettuccine 164

Nachos, Plant 127
noodles
    Asian Noodle Salad 125
    Tofu Noodle Soup 110

oats
    Brooke's Nana Pat's Muesli 87
    Overnight Oats 85
    Peanut Butter and Chocolate Oat Cookies 170
    Yoghurt and oat flatbread 94

Pancakes, Brooke's 83
pasta
    Miso Pumpkin Pasta 144
    Mushroom and Leek Risotto 153
    Mushroom Fettuccine 164
    Ricotta and Spinach Gnocchi 161
peanut butter
    Kate Cambie's Peanut Butter Smoothie 88
    Peanut Butter and Chocolate Oat Cookies 170
    Peanut Butter Date Bliss Balls 180
    Peanut butter sauce 134
Pesto, Basil and Walnut 105
Pickled Eggs on Toast 98
Pickled onion 91
pie
    Kūmara, Lentil and Halloumi Pie 138
    Lentil and Cheese Pie 157
Plant Nachos 127
potatoes
    Jacket Potatoes 120
    Potato and Spinach Frittata 132
Pulled Jackfruit Burgers 137
pumpkin
    Miso Pumpkin Pasta 144
    Pumpkin and Feta Filo Log 122

Raw Carrot Cake 177
Refried beans 127
rice
    Beetroot, Feta and Brown Rice Salad 119
    Coconut rice 167
Ricotta and Spinach Gnocchi 161
Root Vegetable Tagine 151

Saag Paneer 158
salad
    Asian Noodle Salad 125
    Slaw 147
Salsa 140
sauce
    Cheese sauce 157
    Cheesy sauce 127
    Peanut butter sauce 134
    Pumpkin sauce 144
    Tomato zucchini sauce 161
Savoury French Toast 91
seasoning, Mexican 120
Shakshuka with Beans 101
Silken Tofu Mousse 178
Slaw 147
Smoothies 88
    Energiser Smoothie 88
    Green Smoothie 89
    Kate Cambie's Peanut Butter Smoothie 88
soup
    James Coote's Broccoli and Blue Cheese Soup 114
    Super Orange Soup 112
    Tofu Noodle Soup 110
Spicy Chickpea Curry 154
spinach
    Potato and Spinach Frittata 132
    Ricotta and Spinach Gnocchi 161
    Saag Paneer 158
Sprouts 102
Super Orange Soup 112

tacos
    Esther Keown's Crispy Cauli Mexican Tacos 134
Tagine, Root Vegetable 151
tofu
    Hugo Inglis' Black Pepper Mushroom and Tofu 149
    Silken Tofu Mousse 178
    Tofu Noodle Soup 110
tomato
    Tomato Passata 109
    Tomato zucchini sauce 161

Walnut and Basil Pesto 105
wraps
    Egg Breakfast Wraps 92
    Home-made Wraps with Falafel and Greek Yoghurt
        Dressing 130

yoghurt
    Greek yoghurt dressing 130
    Yoghurt and oat flatbread 94

zucchini
    Tomato zucchini sauce 161
    Zucchini Slice 117

Goodbye

We consider ourselves blessed to be elite athletes pursuing our dream jobs.

We are passionate about being good role models to younger athletes, uniting with fellow New Zealanders through sport and all in a way that connects us to the environment.

Our biggest hope for this book is that it will inspire people to think about the choices they make every day. To believe that our decisions, however small, can have an impact. We hope that you take something from this book that will help you, the people around you, your performances, and ultimately make the world a better place.

We also wanted to mention again that we have really enjoyed the process of making this book and we are proud of its contents. We are proud to be donating 100 per cent of the profits to The WaterBoy to help give kids the same opportunities we have had in sport.

All the food photos were taken by Luuka and Brooke at their homes and all of the food has been eaten (even the yuck dishes as we were testing recipes). The recipes have been analysed by Christel to ensure they are good sources of fuel for us.

Thank you for your support and we wish happiness and kindness to you all xx

Acknowledgements

Brooke, Christel and Luuka wish to acknowledge everyone who has played a part in the making of this book. Thank you for being a part of our team.

Pip Arnold, Nick Bartels, Paul Bateman, Madeline Bates, Anna Bruno, Kevin Burgess, Kate Cambie, Tonia Cawood, Sam Charlton, James Coote, Islay Crosbie, Balint Czucz, Marcus Daniel, Leanne Donoghue, Leo Donoghue, Tim Doyle, Juliette Drysdale, Max Dunshea, Steve Dunshea, Tim Dunshea, Jeff Francis, David Galbraith, Kerri Gowler, Lisa Holton, Piera Hudson, Hugo Ingles, Denise Jones, Rod Jones, Esther Keown, Jennifer Kerr, Jackie Kiddle, Justina Kitchen, Sarah-Jane Luoni, Eve Macfarlane, Sophie Mackenzie, Alex Maloney, Ian Mercer, Thomas Nabbs, Brooke Neal, Jennifer Palmer, Georgia Perry, Marlene Perry, Simon Perry, Tiffany Perry, Ashlee Rowe, Louise Russell, Dan Smart, Kate Stace, Courtney Takai, Jon Tanner, Ruby Tui, Mikah Upton, Jim Webster, Linda Webster, Martina Wegman, Kylie Wilson, Graham Windros, Karen Wylaars, Paul Wylaars, Pedro Wylaars, Vincent Wylaars.

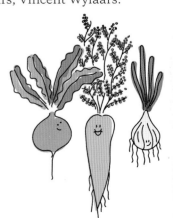